Silver Linings

Friends

Stories to Warm Your Heart

Contributing writers: Gail Cohen, Christine A. Dallman, Margaret Anne Huffman, Marie D. Jones, Karen M. Leet, Ann Russell, Donna Shryer, Diana L. Thrift, Natalie Walker Whitlock

New Seasons is a trademark of Publications International, Ltd.
Copyright © 2002 Publications International, Ltd. All rights reserved. This book may not be reproduced or quoted in whole or in part by any means whatsoever without written permission from:

Louis Weber, CEO
Publications International, Ltd.
7373 North Cicero Avenue
Lincolnwood, Illinois 60712

Permission is never granted for commercial purposes.

Manufactured in China.

8 7 6 5 4 3 2 1

ISBN: 0-7853-4239-7

Library of Congress Card Number: 00-110244

To Laurie
my friend For Life
From Evadene

A good friend makes you feel

like the brightest star in the sky,

the boldest color in a rainbow,

the sweetest flower in a garden.

She finds the best in you

and brings it out for everyone else to see.

Contents

8	True Friends Are Priceless
10	Hero
14	Standing Their Ground
17	An Angel's Dream
21	Handy Mandy
24	New Places, New Traditions
29	Friends Forever
32	Little Clay Pot
36	Risking Friendship Again
40	United We Stand
43	The Grandma Conspiracy
48	The Baby Can't Wait
52	Friend of the Bride
54	Dreams
58	Mac and Me
61	Sophisticated Ladies

64	A Friend in the Family
68	Put on Your Hiking Boots!
70	The Cloudburst
74	Office Mates
77	Visiting Rhoda
80	Date Night
83	I Hear You Loud and Clear
86	Fire Alarm Chili
90	Can You Forgive Me?
93	Miss Priss
97	A Window of Opportunity
100	Paint Job
104	Out of Sight, In My Mind
108	Weigh to Go
112	Unlikely Soul Mates
115	Threesome
117	A Tropical Getaway
120	The Friendship Path
124	Friendship Knows No Age

True Friends Are Priceless

The Bible says that "some friends play at friendship but a true friend sticks closer than one's nearest kin" (Proverbs 18:24). The stories that you are about to read are about "true" friends—people who have our best interests at heart and have touched our lives in unforgettable ways.

Some of these friends are of a different generation, of a different cultural background, and even of a different gender. Yet, however different a friend may be from us, a good friend is someone we will always treasure because they have made us feel valued and understood, and have made our lives richer.

This is not to say, however, that a friend

must be perfect in order to be true. Every relationship has its problems and misunderstandings. In a true and healthy friendship, though, the individuals will work through these difficulties, making the relationship even stronger.

We all yearn for this kind of friendship, especially when the world doesn't seem to be a friendly place. Someone once observed, "A friend is the one who comes in when the whole world has gone out." *Friends: Stories to Warm Your Heart* offers many examples of friends who have "come in" and provided strength, encouragement, insight, and love to someone who needed some light in their world. They will remind you of the friends who have come into your life and will encourage you to be as devoted to your friends.

As you will see as you read the stories in this book, true friends, indeed, are priceless.

Hero

Rhoda and I screamed at the top of our lungs while we floundered our way to shore. Meanwhile, the river carried our canoe toward our destination, a campground ten miles downstream. When Rhoda began to cry, I joined her, hoping someone big and brave would rescue us, but we were out of luck. A darkening sky should have warned us, but it didn't. Adolescents pay little attention to the weather when there are worse problems like wet hair, scraped shins, and wounded pride.

At the tail end of a youth group canoe trip, Rhoda and I had simply let the current carry us. Dawdling, we stopped to poke at water lilies, admire dragon flies, and dangle bare feet in the cool water. Suddenly realizing everyone was out of sight, we dug in our paddles and gave pursuit. Big mistake! We hit a submerged tree, panicked, flipped, and here we were stranded on the banks of a river being dive-bombed by mosquitoes the size of jumbo-jets. The forest was dense with pine trees and low-growing shrubs. The ground beneath our feet was spongy and soft.

"Tree roots," I noted. "They're like big mats. They run under the river. That's how fire can jump across."

I sniffed the air. Was that fire? Or my usual overactive worry button? But when you're a short, skinny nerd who wears wire-rimmed glasses and is called "Runt," you have a lot to worry about. Nevertheless, I smiled, trying not to alarm Rhoda, who was examining a nasty cut on her ankle, probably from a rock. A lonely, shy child, for some reason unclear to me even now, I became the best friend of one of the brightest, funniest kids in our sixth-grade class. To the disdain of her friends, she had invited me on this outing. They had laughed when Rhoda and I nearly tipped as soon as we entered the water because I had oversteered.

"Poor Rhoda," I heard them saying.

I looked at Rhoda with affection and said, "We have to get moving," pulling her to her feet. Checking my compass worn like a rabbit foot on a cord around my neck, I pointed east.

We followed the river, but it wasn't long before I realized Rhoda's ankle was going to slow us down. So we made a crutch from a forked tree branch, padding it with my sweatshirt. A brisk wind cut through my thin T-shirt, and I tried to speed us up. One good thing about being a "nerd" is that you read a lot. I knew that we could stay

warm and dry by weaving grasses and pine boughs around the roots of a fallen tree. Fortunately, we found a good one before darkness settled in. We backed into a small hollow like field mice in a nest. I tried not to think about fire as we stretched out as best we could on the spongy earth floor. For supper, we ate the bounty in my waterproof waist pack. I didn't know about Rhoda's thoughts, but I prayed all night to be delivered from spiders and whatever howled until dawn.

It was years before Rhoda confessed to me that she was sure what she heard that night were vampires stalking their next victim, whom she was sure would be her. She won't believe my claim she slept all night while I kept vigil. It's all part of our legend that grows more terrifying with each telling to our friends, later to our husbands, and now to our children. But what we do agree on is that I had undergone an overnight transformation. When we walked into the ranger's station the next afternoon, I could see by my reflection in the dusty window that I'd grown about 10 feet—at least in the eyes of the kids who usually saw me as a target on which to practice tossing their taunts and barbs. Open-mouthed, they watched as we stumbled from the woods.

"She saved us," Rhoda said, pointing at me with the makeshift crutch.

I have carried the image of me as the "hero" for 40 years. In fact, Rhoda's friendship was the first mirror held up for me to see the person I could grow into. And when I have business setbacks or personal flubs and feel momentarily like the "Runt," I touch that old compass hooked on a chunky silver bracelet Rhoda gave me the year we graduated from college. Holding it, I see again the image of myself her friendship helped form and know I'm heading in the right direction.

A true friend likes you even when you don't like yourself. She will point out all your good qualities and convince you you're worthy of every good thing that happens to you.

Standing Their Ground

My 83-year-old Grandmother Nelly looks like an angel, talks like an angel, and walks like an angel. But watch out, fellas, she's a card shark! And her best pal, Phyllis, is a card shark, too! Nelly and Phyllis are living proof that friendship, like wine, improves with age. They are in great shape and as active and fun-loving as young people, but with none of the baggage that comes with the inexperience of youth. They've got nobody to impress but themselves, and when they sit down at their senior center to play poker with the big guys, look out!

On one particular day, Nelly and Phyllis visit the center to play some cards and get invited to sit at the "big money" table, where the old men eyeball them as if they were aliens. The money they play for is fake, but that doesn't matter to these card sharks, for it's the thrill of winning and the fun of beating their unsuspecting male opponents that counts. Some of the men at the table obviously don't know who the two women are and even talk to them in a conde-

scending fashion as if the women don't have a clue how to play poker. But soon the tables have turned, for by the day's end, Nelly and Phyllis have cleaned the men out and sent them packing!

Excited and more than a bit smug, Nelly and Phyllis begin the walk home to their nearby retirement complex. It is early evening, and the sun has just gone down, but the women feel fairly safe out on the main street of their suburban neighborhood. As they turn down a side street to their complex, they are startled as a man dressed in dark clothing and a ski mask jumps out at them from behind a row of hedges and pushes Phyllis to the ground, then grabs Nelly's purse. She refuses to let go, however, and begins a game of tug of war with the much younger man, who obviously wasn't expecting these old gals to put up such a fight. Meanwhile, Phyllis has gotten herself up off the ground and is flailing the man in the head with her own purse, yelling, screaming, and scolding him as if he were an unruly child.

By this time, several neighbors have come to their aid, and the poor chap is practically tackled by seniors and held down with his face to the ground until police arrive a few minutes later. By this time, a big crowd of onlookers has gathered. Needless to say, when the police remove the man's ski mask, his face is red with embarrassment as he

is dragged into the waiting police car, and there are Nelly and Phyllis still scolding him and shaking their fingers at him. Although the officers tell them they are lucky to still be in one piece, the two women do have their purses, and their pride. The police commend them and other seniors for capturing a man they say is a suspect in four muggings in the area during the past few weeks.

The next day, Nelly and Phyllis are celebrities at the center, even making the front page of the local community newspaper, but they are too busy playing cards and shutting down the competition to even care about their newfound notoriety. And from now on, when they walk home after a long day of card sharking, they carry their purses close to their bodies, their heads held high and aware, and their alarm whistles around their necks. Sometimes, they even let two lucky men from the center walk them home.

An Angel's Dream

I first met Elizabeth in March of 1994. I had been a host mother for foreign students studying English in California, and most of my previous students had been women in their twenties. Elizabeth, though—a woman from Germany—was 51. I wondered how it would be having a strange woman close to my own age staying in my home for one month.

When the doorbell rang, I felt nervous. Yet, when I saw her smiling face and twinkling eyes, my skepticism disappeared. I hugged her and welcomed her into my home, and from that instant we were close friends.

Each morning we shared breakfast together, and then she'd be off to her classes. In the afternoon, she would come home, and we'd talk about our lives for hours over tea. She told me that her husband had died the year before. He had lost a lot of money in a failed business venture and jumped from a building to his death. Elizabeth's son

and daughter took their father's suicide extremely hard and became estranged from her, somehow blaming her for his death.

She missed her two children dearly and often talked of her hope of reconciliation, but meanwhile she had been pouring her love out to mentally and physically disabled children. She told me she considered these children her precious "angels" and that her work made her happy, but that there would always be a hole in her heart for her own children.

In turn, Elizabeth proved to be a caring listener when I would tell her about my three precious children, and also when I poured out my grief and anger over the breakup of my marriage a few years before. We took turns listening, advising, and supporting.

Recently, Elizabeth had a breast removed due to cancer, and she confided in me that even though she felt and looked fine on the outside, she was afraid no man would accept her disfigured body. I told her any man would be lucky to have an angel like her. It seemed we could talk to each other about anything.

Sometimes Elizabeth would come home with a gift for me, usually something beautiful and blue, my favorite color, or a lovely picture

frame for my cherished family photos. I would often be shopping and see a beautiful angel statuette or doll, and it immediately reminded me of Elizabeth and her precious disabled "angels." She would practically squeal with delight when I presented her with these angel gifts.

One afternoon, Elizabeth shared her one big dream with me. She hoped someday she could open a home for her disabled angels, a home where they could be happy and cared for and surrounded with love. I held her hand and told her I believed in her and that her wish would come true if she really believed in it. I could see the gratitude in her eyes.

The month passed quickly, and soon we were standing in the airport in tears hugging each other good-bye. We exchanged farewell gifts, and as she boarded her plane, I felt as if half of my own heart was leaving with her.

Over the next few months we were in constant contact. Elizabeth wanted to send me a ticket to come to Germany, but because of my other students I was unable to leave. I promised I'd come visit soon, though. A few months later, I received a letter that gave me joy. Elizabeth had finally confronted her son and daughter, and they had

all broken down in tears of grief that soon turned to healing and reconciliation. One of her dreams had come true, just like we had hoped.

Elizabeth's other dream also came true about a year later. She sent a photo of a house she had purchased and converted into a home for her disabled angels. She was unbelievably happy and full of new passion for life.

Then one day I received a card in the mail. It was in German, and I couldn't understand it, except for one word—the German word for "bereaved." My heart sank. The card was signed by Elizabeth's two children. I asked one of my other German students to translate the card while I fought back the tears. This vibrant, loving, beautiful woman had died. Her breast cancer had returned with a sudden swiftness that gave her little time to contact friends. I spent the next few days grieving and sent her children a card to try to express what words could not express—how much I loved their mother and how much I would miss her.

When I was able to stop grieving, I remembered all that she was and all that she had done in her life. She had fulfilled her dreams, and now her love and light were needed elsewhere. The woman who loved angels was now an angel herself.

Handy Mandy

"Here I am, Scaredy-Cat," my best friend called through the screen door. "I'm all set to move in for the weekend and protect you until Bob gets back."

"I don't need protecting," I protested. "It's just that I'm not used to being alone here—"

"In the big bad suburbs!" Mandy joked.

"Well, you never know what could go wrong." I held the door open for her as she hauled in a suitcase. "I'm not very good with emergencies. What if the pilot light went out or the electricity went off?"

Mandy laughed. "The world would come to an end!"

"Anyway, it's great to have you over. It'll be like the sleepovers we had when we were kids."

We had a wonderful evening curled up in comforters in front of the TV, but later Mandy called out from the bathroom, "Ginny, your sink seems to be clogged up."

"I know," I answered, obviously exasperated. "We've been having some trouble with it lately."

"Do you have any drain unclogging stuff?"

"There's a bottle in the cabinet," I replied.

The next morning Mandy wanted to know where Bob's toolbox was. "It's in the basement," I told her with a puzzled look. "What do you want it for?"

"Your drain is still clogged," she said. "I'm going to tighten up your faucets."

Later I heard ominous noises—tools clanking, water running, and Mandy muttering to herself.

"What's going on in there?"

"Nothing. Do you have a coat hanger? I've got your drain almost cleaned out, and I'm starting on the faucet."

"Are you sure you know what you're doing?"

"Of course. I fix things all the time," she answered with obvious confidence.

There was a sudden loud gushing sound from the bathroom. Mandy rushed out, looking extremely upset. "I can't believe it! Something went wrong in there," she panted.

Was she ever right! The thing that went wrong was . . . Mandy. As the plumber later explained, Mandy had poured an entire bottle of corrosive drain cleaner into a plastic pipe, which promptly melted. Then she jammed a coat hanger into it to "finish" cleaning it out. A hole was the natural result, but Mandy didn't notice this until she tightened the faucet, which broke and refused to shut off. By then water was spraying out everywhere.

I found an emergency plumbing service, mopped up the mess, and comforted my hysterical friend by taking her out for a hot fudge sundae. I'm glad Mandy came to stay with me that weekend. Now I know when to call a plumber and when to call a friend.

Friendships are like flowers—some last a few days, some last much longer. The best ones will thrive if they're given tender loving care.

New Places, New Traditions

"Life's a trade-off," Nancy reminded herself while she navigated her car through unfamiliar streets. Bad job/good job. Small apartment/half a house. But Georgia sunshine for Massachusetts snow? Nancy shook her head at her folly, peering into the swirling snow searching for landmarks. The three children sat quietly behind her, exhausted beyond squabbling.

"The good news is we have a place to live," Nancy said, trying for cheerfulness in the spirit of the season. The town looked like a Christmas card now that Thanksgiving had passed, except for one dark house among a block of stately homes.

Nancy's heart sank as she turned into the driveway. The porch light came on, and an older woman peered over the porch railing while Nancy and her kids slowly emerged from the car.

"You're late," the woman noted sternly, which made all four feel awkward and very unwanted.

"We got stuck in a snow drift," Nancy replied anxiously, wanting to soften the woman's apparent anger.

"It takes hearty souls to live here. Come along then." With that, the woman abruptly led them into the first floor of the house. Recently widowed, Josephine was reluctantly "taking in boarders," as she preferred to call it. In reality, her family home had been divided into two spacious apartments. The loveliness of the home brought tears to Nancy's eyes. Pristine hardwood floors and woodwork, tall ceilings, the aroma of lemon polish that'd kept built-in cupboards and bookcases  gleaming a hundred years. The parlor had been converted into two bedrooms, the living room into another bedroom and a den. The kitchen, with glass-fronted cupboards, held a small round oak table and four chairs.

"My family and I always sat there. I couldn't change it," said Josephine. She turned away and then paused at the foot of a back staircase. "The doctors and my busybody children say I have to leave

my door unlocked in case I have another spell. I don't plan to. I'll not bother you, and I expect the same. Good night."

During a blizzard, movers carried in furniture that'd been in Nancy's family, as well as what she'd collected and restored. They looked immediately at home. She registered the kids at their new school and was welcomed with open arms at the teaching hospital. At home, however, a chill remained. Josephine avoided contact except when there was something to complain about, like new sleds parked too close to the driveway or a noisy snowball fight. Subsequently, the children hid when they saw her coming, and she turned down Nancy's invitation for coffee and a chance to see how beautifully things fit. Among the last boxes Nancy and the children unpacked were the Christmas decorations. Homesickness descended like fog.

"New places, new traditions," Nancy coaxed her children, reaching for a wreath to hang. After decorating, they gathered around the old oak table, laughing, reminiscing, and dreaming. Overhead, Josephine walked in sharp paces, disapprovingly it seemed, in her apartment. Seen from the street, its darkness was in sharp contrast with the

downstairs, now gaily lit with candles at the windows, handmade decorations, and a towering tree, which brushed against the 12-foot ceiling. *Not like home with Magnolia leaves, pepperberries, and fresh holly*, Nancy thought, *but the weary, lonely heart accepts what is offered.* She was leaving for work when she heard Josephine on the porch talking to the postal carrier.

"No, it certainly isn't a merry Christmas," Josephine muttered, "and I'm most definitely not going to decorate this year."

The poor carrier fled, as Nancy leaned against the door, out of sight. She recognized loneliness when she met it, for it was lodged in her heart, too.

"Get in the car," Nancy called to her children that afternoon, pulling up beside them as they walked home from school. "We've got Christmas mischief to pull."

As soon as Josephine left for choir practice that evening, they raced upstairs carrying the small tree and ornaments they'd bought. Taking a deep breath, they entered the forbidden but unlocked connecting door into Josephine's apartment. In record time, they set up the tiny tree, its colored lights twinkling bravely against the darkened windows. They were eating supper when Josephine returned, trudging upstairs. They held their breath. Yet nothing happened. Nancy's heart sank. "At least the tree didn't come flying out a window," she told the children.

They discovered an invitation under the backstairs door the next morning. "Supper tonight," and it was signed "Josephine." At the bottom was a poignant postscript, "Please come."

The house smelled of baking bread when Nancy and the children climbed the stairs that evening. After vegetable soup and homemade French bread, Josephine, at the children's insistence, carried out the old manger scene she'd just happened to mention. And then there were the hand-carved reindeer that needed to come out of the attic.

Soup supper like the one they'd celebrated that night became one of their many traditions, melding generations and families. A celebration of sharing space and gifts—the most precious, a friendship that glows more brightly for Nancy, the children, and Josephine, who's now more like a granny than a landlady with each passing year.

Friends Forever

I stood staring down at the letter clutched in my hand, and I felt an aching deep down inside me.

"Oh, no," I whispered, tears pouring down my face. A dozen memories flooded my mind. We'd been best friends from grade school right on through college. I couldn't even recall all the times we'd been together, all the experiences we'd shared, all the moments that held special meaning for our friendship.

How had we drifted apart? We'd gone our separate ways, choosing husbands, settling in widely distant states, becoming absorbed in the hectic schedules of being wives and moms. We'd kept in touch, of course, but we'd lost that closeness, that oneness of being best friends. Sure, we still exchanged cards for birthdays and Christmas, but our notes were full of superficial comments—nothing deep, nothing real.

But not this letter crumpled now in my grasp. Not this letter. My mind bobbed wildly over the years. Back in grade school, we'd worked hard for high grades and didn't always fit in with those who didn't work hard. All through junior high, we wore plaid skirts and

twin sweater sets and walked together to football games. In high school we'd shared giggles and hopes during endless phone calls, sighing over appealing teen boys who had caught our hearts.

In college we'd loved riding together in my dad's flashy convertible—with the top down, of course. I suppose we started the slow drift apart then, while our majors and interests pushed us further away from one another. Still, we'd found time for late night stops at the snack bar for hot fudge sundaes, then quick jogs around the circle to work off the extra calories.

We'd still talk as we rode together to classes, sharing hopes, dreams, worries, and fears. We knew each other so well. We enjoyed the same music, liked the same clothing styles, and used the same gift bow on packages exchanged between us for years, one of our favorite ongoing jokes.

Now, after long years apart, separated by miles and differing lifestyles, my heart melted for my friend. She'd lost a child, and my whole being yearned to be with her. This was the worst sort of pain I could imagine. This was devastating. I flew out immediately to be with her. During my flight, I had time to wonder whether too many years had passed, if too many differences had come between us.

But we hugged as if nothing had changed, as if no time had passed. We clung together and wept, her pain as raw and grating as if it were

my own. The years fell away, and I thought of her as the girl I'd grown up with, the friend who'd stood by me through a thousand rough moments, the pal as close as any sister could have been.

Somehow she got through those terrible days, though I knew as sure as I knew anything that nothing would ever take away the pain she carried within her. That kind of loss never completely fades.

Since then our letters, exchanged over the miles that separate us still, touch a deeper chord. At holidays, I think of her and of the loss that aches inside her, and I pray for her as I write a loving note or send an encouraging Scripture verse. And I believe that somehow nothing will come between us and the friendship we have always shared—not distance, not work, not time. Some people are meant to be friends forever, and nothing can change that.

Though we may be many miles apart,
the ribbon of your friendship binds my heart.

Little Clay Pot

My friend Dorothy and I had been traveling together in my old green van for almost two weeks. We'd begun in Southern California, driven up the coast into Washington to the foot of the still smoldering Mount St. Helens, then through Idaho and Montana into Yellowstone, with its cascading hot springs and grizzly bears. We had just stopped for the night in Cody, Wyoming, taken in the rodeo, and booked adjoining rooms at the historic Irma, built in 1902 by Buffalo Bill Cody and named after his youngest daughter.

It was a great trip, but we'd never been alone together for that long before—driving, camping, eating, talking, shopping, looking at maps—and, not surprisingly, we had started to get on each other's nerves. It did not help that she was sometimes indirect, and I was sometimes dense. I guess it had to come to a head, and finally it did.

I'd planned to roll out of Cody after breakfast and was anxious to get on the road, but Dorothy wanted to spend the morning at the Plains Indian Museum. She'd mentioned it the night before, but I'd

underestimated how much she really wanted to go. I suppose I thought she'd give in if I said we didn't have time. Usually I'm as spontaneous as anyone else, but that morning I was out of sorts. I didn't realize until later that I was simply a little homesick. So I pushed my agenda—hard, but for once, she pushed back.

Well, I gave in, but not without acting like a colossal idiot. I drove her to the museum, but then refused to go in—ostensibly because it cost a few dollars.

"I can't see paying for such a short visit!" I fumed. I lurked outside for a couple of hours while she wandered inside, enthralled by the museum's art and artifacts.

When she emerged, she was at peace, radiating an inner light stimulated by the beauty she'd encountered. I was sorry I'd missed my chance to go with her, sorry I'd acted so stubborn, and sorry I'd almost deprived her of this experience. We smiled at each other, awkwardly at first, then conspiratorially while she handed me her ticket.

"You can't leave here without at least seeing the sculpture of the woman in the courtyard—you'll really like it," she whispered, and then she sent me in with instructions about what to see along the way.

Unchallenged by the guard, who wouldn't have been the first to mistake me for Dorothy, I walked quickly through the halls, past rooms filled with tipis, exhibits, and artwork I had allowed myself no time to see. I found the courtyard and the sculpture, and did, indeed, appreciate the flowing lines of the woman's robes and the integrity and strength in her face.

Because there was no charge for the gift shop, we went in together. I browsed while she examined a collection of little clay pots. Each was unique, a treasure signed by the artist. She chose an especially lovely one with a little ebony inlaid stone; it was smaller than the palm of her hand. I almost gasped when I heard the price, but Dorothy asked the clerk to wrap it carefully, and taking it, we left Cody.

The rest of the trip was all right, and I think I ran roughshod over her wishes only one other time before we made it home.

After two decades, our friendship has endured, surviving a misunderstanding here, a disappointment there, but much more often giving each of us enjoyment, under-standing, and respect. A couple of years ago, she brought out the

tiny clay pot, which she usually kept safely behind glass. We reminisced about our trip, about how glad we were that we did it, especially since we both had acquired too many responsibilities to even think of doing such a thing again anytime soon.

"Don't you remember," she asked me, "the trip was your idea?"

"Well, I don't recall having to work too hard to talk you into it," I answered, laughing.

"I'm so glad I went," she told me, giving me a hug. "You know, when I bought that little pot in Cody, I wasn't sure how much longer we'd be friends. Then, when we got back, I decided I would leave it to you in my will!" She laughed at my shock. "But, you know, I'd rather give this clay pot to you now. Here," she said, handing it to me.

I started to protest. "Why—" Why would she want to give me this after my boorish behavior at the museum that day?

Yet, when I looked into her tawny eyes, I could see what the gift was truly honoring—not merely our trip, that wonderful adventure—but our friendship, a friendship that would outlast all sorts of foolish mistakes.

Risking Friendship Again

When I met Lindsay, we were each struggling—somewhat alone—in our difficulties. Of course, everyone struggles. It's a fact of life. But Lindsay's situation was epic. A betrayal by those whom she considered her best friends had turned her world upside down and had nearly torn apart her marriage and family. When our paths crossed, she was still deeply wounded and understandably guarded.

As for me, I was feeling as if my soul had been thrown into the trunk of a car, taken to "no-man's land," and dumped there. I was floundering badly in many areas of my life, not the least of which was my career. Self-doubt and frustration were sabotaging my dreams of building a freelance writing career. Pressure from others to "get a real job" increasingly tormented me, suffocating my lifelong hope. I was tiptoeing around the edges of despair, and I felt terribly alone.

So there we were—in such states of heart and mind—when circumstances arranged our introduction and orchestrated the beginnings of our friendship. A fantastic musician, Lindsay, along with her husband and children, had been visiting at the church I attended. She had no idea how desperately I had prayed for someone with her musical expertise to come along. Just prior to her arrival, I had been handed the job of leading the congregational singing. However, I was inexperienced in planning services and had been scrambling each week to put together some semblance of a music program that would flow well.

When Lindsay learned that I was looking for help, she agreed to give me a hand. Though I did not know it at the time, this was a courageous step for her. Displacement from her role in a music group (through no fault of her own) had been one of the blows she'd been dealt in the fallout of broken trust. Helping me plan this program would be the first time in more than two years that she had used her musical skills.

Lindsay and I began to work together. As we did, the seeds of our friendship were planted ever so cautiously. I had grown weary of having my dreams scoffed at, and Lindsay was not about to play the

fool by trusting too easily or too soon. However, an irresistible camaraderie began to take us both by surprise.

In spite of her own damaged ideals, I discovered that Lindsay still believed in reaching for them, in recovering them. *Hope* was a word she used again and again in our conversations. My listless morale and wilting confidence revived when I spent time talking with her. And I was so starved for positive messages that I found myself looking for excuses to visit her home and share her company.

Lindsay's encouragement was a catalyst to begin the healing of my soul's malady, but hers was not so easily mended. Trust is built over time. Only time could determine whether my friendship was trustworthy. Yet only eight months after we had met, Lindsay surprised me one day with a courageous offer: Would I come live in her home, rent free, in exchange for my doing housework and other errands? She believed in my goal of becoming a full-time writer. Living with her family would give me the financial freedom to continue reaching for that goal. Conversely, my help around the house would make it possible for her to begin a new, in-home sewing business while she also kept up with three very socially active and sports-involved children.

I hesitated. I did not want to tax this friendship and risk losing it. Nor did I ever want to give her cause to wonder if her trust had been broken in any way. We talked about these things, acknowledged the existing risk, worked out some parameters in which to live, and took hold of hope.

My living quarters were a rather large laundry room. Because of that, my nickname became "Lint-erella," and I became part of the family. It was the most wonderful time of my life. After two years in Lindsay's home, I was able to head out on my own as a full-time writer. Today I am living out my dream.

During that time, Lindsay and I cemented a special confidence and trust in each other. We both know that healing and blessing came to each of us when we needed it most. And we thank God for that.

As I look back and consider my friend's bold step in helping me along, I am moved by her courage. Today our relationship remains strong. Its roots run deep, like a tree that has grown up out of a rich soil of hope—hope that was willing to risk, trusting that friendship might grow once again.

United We Stand

There is nothing like a good friend to cheer you up when life gets you down. For Callie, that friend was Gina, her coworker at a large insurance company. They were both attractive, friendly, and single, and they often shared horror stories about bad blind dates and encounters with Mr. Wrong.

The two women had met on Gina's first day on the job, when she literally ran into Callie with an enormous stack of office documents. While they were picking up the papers, they both saw a gorgeous young man come into the office to meet with his agent. Dumbstruck, they both stood there staring at him until another coworker passed by and asked them if they were all right. They looked at each other and then burst into laughter. And so a strong friendship was born, sparking numerous meetings in the ladies' room, which then became lunches, then actual get-togethers where either Callie or Gina would cook dinner as the

other told a long tale of woe about the previous night's date from hell.

At work, they even managed to be assigned to the same department, and it was only through sheer willpower that they ever got any work done in between their chat sessions. When Gina picked up the flu and was out for over a week, Callie took on her friend's workload and brought chicken soup and plenty of office gossip to ease Gina's pain.

Nevertheless, their friendship was tested when they visited a new restaurant that had opened next door to their office building and saw the most gorgeous waiter on earth. His name was Dominic, and he was the epitome of tall, dark, and handsome. Callie and Gina were both sure he was Mr. Right; thus began a competition to get his attention that started out friendly, but by lunch's end, had become a little more serious than they had expected. As they left the restaurant to go back to the office, there was a tension between them that neither had experienced before, perhaps because they had never been in competition for a man's attention before. Neither one mentioned the waiter for the rest of the day.

The next day, Callie asked Gina what her plans were for lunch. Gina said she had a doctor's appointment, so would have to skip it. Imagine how surprised Callie was when she went to the same

restaurant as the day before and saw Gina there, chatting with the cute waiter! And Gina was just as surprised to see Callie there, for she could have sworn Callie had told her she was going to eat at her desk and keep working.

After a few days of not speaking to each other, Callie and Gina ran into each other in the crowded ladies room. Callie ignored Gina, and vice versa, and they were both about to leave and go their separate ways when they overheard two of their coworkers telling a third gal about the shy, mousy new girl in Accounting—the one who they all couldn't believe was engaged to be married to that hunk of a waiter, Dominic, at the restaurant next door.

It took all Callie and Gina had to keep them from simultaneously bursting out in laughter. While they stumbled outside, they rushed back to their desks and fell into their chairs in a fit of giggles. As they shook their heads in amused disbelief, Callie suggested they do lunch at another restaurant down the street. Gina smiled and agreed, and on the way over to that restaurant, they laughed and promised each other that never again would a man, no matter how gorgeous, come between them.

Friends like you don't happen along every day. I'm glad you happened to me.

The Grandma Conspiracy

"He's been at it again!" Mrs. Wilkins wailed. "How are we ever going to stop this?"

Mrs. Wilkins and Mrs. Crowe had just returned from their Thursday trip to the mall to find that the neighborhood vandal had struck again. Half-a-dozen black-eyed Susans had been snapped off in Mrs. Wilkins's borders and were strewn across the sidewalk leading up to her townhouse. Next door at Mrs. Crowe's place, marigolds had been beheaded, and handfuls of the beautiful ivy that trailed from her window box had been yanked out.

"It's happened to us four times now," Mrs. Crowe moaned. "It's so upsetting!"

"Well, the police won't help," Mrs. Wilkins said. "Last time I called them, they said it was probably just kids in the neighborhood. They weren't about to send out a squad car to protect some flower beds."

"Then we'll have to catch whoever it is ourselves! Tomorrow we'll watch from behind those bushes, and then we'll grab him!"

Mrs. Wilkins blanched. "What do you mean, *grab*? For heaven's sake, Sara, we're a couple of old ladies!"

The next afternoon, however, they crouched uncomfortably among the shrubs for quite awhile. Mrs. Wilkins was just about to say it was all nonsense when they both heard footsteps. Then there was a sudden crash. The two friends leapt out of the bushes just in time to see a small boy in a red T-shirt running away.

"Why, it's little Dustin Walker! Dustin, you come back here!" Mrs. Crowe called out, but he vanished around the corner. Both women stared at the broken crock of geraniums on Mrs. Crowe's sidewalk and then back toward the corner. Mrs. Crowe knew she'd have to call Dustin's mother.

That evening the two friends sat together on Mrs. Crowe's patio, sipping tea.

"Dustin's mother was upset when I told her about the trouble he's been causing," Mrs. Crowe said. "She told me she can't afford to pay for an after-school baby-sitter. Dustin is supposed to come straight home and stay inside until she gets out of work, but, of course, he doesn't and usually manages to get into trouble."

"He must feel lonely coming into an empty house after school. Maybe he's even afraid to stay at home by himself," Mrs. Wilkins suggested. "Of course, he's still done some very bad things, but I can't help feeling a bit sorry for him."

"Martha Jane . . . I think I've come up with a great idea. Why don't we adopt him?"

"What? You're crazy, Sara Crowe!"

"Not legally, Martha Jane. I mean we could become his adoptive grandmas. He needs an extended family, and, well, we haven't got anything more important to do, have we?" She waited as her friend mulled this over.

Mrs. Wilkins gave a long sigh. "I guess I'd better call my grandson and find out what six-year-old boys are interested in nowadays."

The next afternoon they kept an eye out for Dustin. As he walked by, slowly heading for the empty townhouse, Mrs. Wilkins called out to him.

"Hi, Dustin. That's a nice T-shirt."

"Huh?" Dustin answered in surprise. He looked at the two women, expecting a tongue-lashing for his recent mischief.

"We just baked some chocolate chip cookies," Mrs. Crowe said. "Why don't you come in and have some? My grandchildren left a *Lion King* video here last time they visited."

"Your mom said it would be OK," Mrs. Wilkins added.

The smell of freshly baked cookies hung in the air. "Well, I guess I can come in for a little while," Dustin decided.

He wasn't sure what to make of them at first, and he didn't let his guard down all at once. But they were always interested in hearing about school, the games he liked to play, and his friends. Soon he found himself stopping at Mrs. Crowe's townhouse after school without even thinking about it. By now they had a used video game player and a pile of games from Mrs. Wilkins's grandchildren, along with several movies on tape from Mrs. Crowe's family. Then when they started buying model airplane and car kits, Dustin was truly

fascinated. He'd never tried to make anything like a model before. The two ladies helped Dustin understand the directions; he spent many contented hours gluing and painting.

"Could I invite my friends over tomorrow?" Dustin asked one afternoon. "I showed them some of my models, and they want to try making one." Mrs. Crowe and Mrs. Wilkins exchanged triumphant glances. The Grandma Conspiracy had worked. They were now a part of Dustin's life.

From that day on, Mrs. Crowe's townhouse was filled with bustle and laughter every weekday afternoon as three little boys played and chattered and ate cookies. The only exceptions were when an important soccer match was taking place at the elementary school. On those afternoons Mrs. Crowe and Mrs. Wilkins brought folding chairs to the field, where they watched the game and cheered whenever Dustin, Mikey, or Corey was in the game. And whenever Dustin was asked about the two silver-haired ladies who attended all his important school events, he answered happily, "Those are my grandmas—I've got two of 'em!"

Friendship is a flower that blooms through all life's seasons.

The Baby Can't Wait!

This was it! Denise knew the instant heavy contractions gripped her body that this baby was on its way *right now.* After three weeks of false alarms, it was about time. Only Denise and her husband, Tim, had gotten careless. Neither was ready. Tim had gone on to work, and it would be at least 20 minutes before he could get home, even if he left immediately.

Dropping into a chair, Denise clutched the chair arms. Suddenly she felt she didn't have 20 minutes. The contractions were only a few minutes apart.

"Oh, my gosh, the baby's coming," she muttered aloud.

"What Mom? Is the baby coming?" her young daughter demanded eagerly. Meanwhile, her small son whooped with excitement and

began racing circles around the room, chanting, "Baby's coming! Baby's coming!"

"Call Mrs. Baker," Denise told her daughter, pressing one fist hard against her throbbing back. "Hurry!" *Mustn't panic. Stay calm. Got to hang on.*

"Call anytime if you need us," Holly had offered from next door. They were good friends, sharing fun times and swapping stories about their kids.

In just moments Holly and Jack dashed through the doorway. Holly took one look at Denise and rounded up the kids, instructing Jack to quickly get the van.

"Have you called Tim?" Holly asked, while Denise leaned back against the chair, tensing from a very strong contraction. After Denise nodded, Holly gently inquired, "How far apart are the contractions?"

"Seven minutes," Denise muttered, "and getting stronger."

Holly herded the kids toward the door. "Let's get the kids settled at my house, Denise. We'll take you to the hospital if Tim doesn't get here soon."

Denise felt calmer already with Holly there, and with Jack beside her so solid and steady. Holly looked as if she was directing traffic, sending children in one direction and her husband toward the garage. Denise, on the other hand, was concentrating on having a baby. *Breathe, two, three, four. Stay calm, relax.* Even after having two already, giving birth to a baby was no picnic. She felt immensely thankful for Holly and Jack. They'd help get her through it.

As Holly eased her toward their van, Denise heard tires squealing, and there was Tim in record time. Holly and Jack got her inside the car, and Denise and Tim took off, knowing the kids were in good hands as they saw their neighbors waving from the driveway.

Though Denise could hardly believe it, they made it to the hospital in time to deliver a healthy baby boy with hardly any complications. But she wouldn't ever want to cut it that close again. An orderly had raced her down the hall, desperate to get her to the delivery room.

Later, Holly and Jack showed up to visit, bringing Denise's excited children. While the kids climbed up to snuggle close to Denise, and Jack shook hands with Tim, Holly stood there grinning happily.

"What are you grinning about?" Denise asked. "I did all the work."

"Oh, nothing," Holly told her. "I'm just very, very glad Tim showed up when he did. I really didn't think you were going to be able to

wait much longer. I told Jack that I thought we might wind up delivering that baby right there on your living room floor! But, hey, if you can't call your friend to drop by and deliver your baby, what kind of a friendship is it?" Then she leaned around the children, and the two women hugged, their cheeks glistening with tears.

"I owe you a box of chocolate cigars," Denise whispered.

Holly responded with a huge smile. "Don't worry, you just might get the chance to do the same for me," and she patted her own tummy.

Your silent companionship is often more healing than words of advice.

Friend of the Bride

I struggled with whether I should have come back for Rachel's wedding, but a promise made is a promise kept, despite scandal. I'd chosen to leave town last year to avoid a community that no longer wanted me to teach its students even though it was my husband—my ex-husband—who, as the school district treasurer, had run away with the building fund.

"You're being tarred by the same brush," fumed my friend Jillian when she hugged me good-bye. "It's not fair."

The day the school board suggested I resign, Jillian and I vowed not to let this interfere with our friendship of 15 years. While Jillian was a single parent with five children, I'd been a teacher to hundreds, including Jillian's.

When the wedding march began, I gathered my thoughts and stood tall. While I smoothed my hair and my long magenta gown, the organ music swelled. Smiling over the head of Rachel, Jillian's oldest daughter, Jillian and I began our triumphal entry arm in arm with the bride.

"Her father would've loved you standing in for him," Jillian whispered. "Let the busybodies talk." And they did, but more about the bride walking between friends who loved her and one another.

Advising the bride and groom, the minister told them to value and nurture their friendship most of all. Then the minister remarked, "Friendship can be more powerful than blood bonds and can bridge time, distance, and trouble. Protect and guard this bond so that what was formed in your youth will only grow stronger as the years pass."

A year later, I returned. Jillian had called to say, "Rachel wants you here. And I need you."

Once again we each stood on either side of Rachel, where Jillian and I shared another precious moment meant to be shared with those we love. After a mighty push, Rachel gave birth to a healthy, beautiful baby.

My new husband had waited in the hospital lobby. Jillian had been an attendant, and our bulletin had listed her simply as "Friend of the Bride." And in our vows, I'd told my new beloved what I'd learned with Jillian—that friendship is a sturdy craft in which to travel into the future.

Dreams

Friends don't let friends give up on their dreams. Such was the case for Lisa and Carrie, two very different people from very different backgrounds. Lisa was slim, beautiful, and upbeat, always giving off positive energy. She came from a tight, loving family. It seemed to Carrie that Lisa had everything going for her. Carrie, on the other hand, was struggling with obesity and depression, which often kept her from doing the things she knew would get her healthy again. Her past was filled with abuse and various family problems, and she frequently felt lost in the world and bitter about her upbringing.

When they met on the job, Carrie loved Lisa's energy and kindness, and Lisa got a kick out of Carrie's wry humor and humility, and the two quickly became close friends. Their boss was an abusive woman, and they would sit for hours gossiping and making fun of the evil woman when she was out of the office. But that was not the only thing that they had in common. It was a similar dream of

becoming successful writers that surmounted all their differences and created an instant bond of friendship.

As they learned more and more about each other, they realized that they must have been brought together by some higher force, for both had been having serious doubts about their writing. Now, they each had a kindred spirit to talk to and share their hopes and fears with, in between working hard on the job and trying to satisfy a boss who refused to be satisfied. It gave them both something to look forward to each morning.

They read each other's work and offered support and encouragement, which each of them desperately needed. With Lisa's help, Carrie even landed an agent for her romance novel and mustered up the courage and self-confidence to start writing poetry again, her true calling. Lisa was inspired to finish a project she had been sitting on for years, thanks to Carrie's gentle nudging. Just having someone else believe in them, and their talent, made both women realize how precious friendship can be and how true caring and love can transcend any physical, religious, or economical differences between people. It was a friendship that proved so strong that they both stuck

it out on the job so they could spend time together. And every moment the boss was away from the office, they would find each other and sit and work and talk and laugh and dream.

They kept each other going during many hard times, like when Carrie suffered from debilitating depression, marriage problems, and troubles with their unsympathetic boss, and when Lisa floundered financially and struggled with caring for her alcoholic husband. When Carrie was down, Lisa lifted her up. When Lisa found it difficult to carry on, Carrie rattled off reasons why she should. The value of their friendship really hit home when a third woman at the office, Anita, whom Carrie and Lisa had both grown close to, suddenly died of heart failure at the age of 25. They realized just how fragile and precious each day of their lives truly was—an insight that convinced both that they must go after their dreams and not wait another moment. For the untimely death of their mutual friend reminded them there are not many moments to spare.

It was at that point that Lisa decided to follow her heart, even if it led her to another city, away from Carrie. She made plans to move back home to where her extended family was and begin writing as a career, a move that would require more faith and courage than she had alone. Although saddened, Carrie was fully supportive. She knew that true friendship meant wanting what is best for the other person, even if that means they have to leave. At

the same time, Carrie vowed to straighten out her home life and even began to look for a new job with a more supportive boss. She also started sending out poems and short stories while she worked hard on her second romance novel. Though they would no longer be seeing each other every day, the bond continued via phone calls, e-mails, and prayers. And they both kept writing.

Had Lisa and Carrie not found their way to each other—to volley support and encouragement to each other, to read each other's work and share ideas, and to just believe in each other when confidence was a scarce commodity—neither of them would have stuck with their difficult dreams. And neither of them would be experiencing the success they have today, as prolific, published writers, proving that sometimes two pairs of wings are better than one for flying high and reaching your dreams.

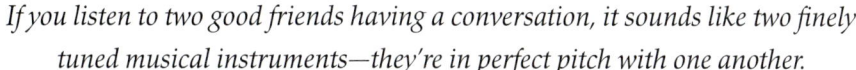

If you listen to two good friends having a conversation, it sounds like two finely tuned musical instruments—they're in perfect pitch with one another.

Mac and Me

After my husband, Jim, passed away, I lived in our rambling ranch-style house in the suburbs alone. There were many inevitable adjustments for me to make—the big ones, of course, but also the small, trivial ones. Some I had not anticipated, nor even thought about. One of those adjustments was assuming the responsibility for the yard work.

My husband and I had used a weekly lawn and landscaping service for many years, but now that extra help became a luxury I would have to do without. Yet, I could manage the work myself. As Jim would have said, "It's not rocket science, Maisy." I took my time getting prepared and read the owner's manuals. I had the equipment serviced. Then, I began to mow the yard, trim the hedges, and tackle the job of cleanup. Soon I could handle the trimmer and mower like a pro.

Still, my age and the accompanying infirmities took their toll on my body. Much to my chagrin, I had to stop and rest frequently. It was a strenuous task, even for a person half my age, I told myself as I worked. What seemed like fun at first became increasingly a drudgery I did not look forward to.

I noticed that my young neighbor walked her dog early every morning, during approximately the same time that I chose to mow my yard. Though we had never been friendly before, she began to speak to me. First, it was just a cordial smile and a wave. After several weeks, she came close enough to be heard over the drone of the mower and commented on the impressive job I was doing. Soon she would stop and visit with me every week, and I welcomed the brief respite from my labor. She then introduced me to her dog, Lady, adding that her name was Mac, short for Mackenzie.

As the cool spring turned into warm summer days, the work took longer and was more difficult; my rests came closer together. Then, my visits with Mac became even more eagerly awaited. I would turn off the mower when I saw her approaching. Although there were more than 50 years between us, we had similar thoughts on politics, the same taste in movies, and the same "old-fashioned" values. And, much to my surprise, I discovered that Mac had a delightful sense of humor about the foibles of youth and the ironies of age.

One morning, the loud and distinctive whir of a motor woke me up. I was alarmed, as the sound seemed to be

coming from somewhere very close to my house. I quickly looked out my window to see what was making the noise. To my surprise and delight, my young friend was mowing my yard!

It was only the first of many times she did this, during which our long and dear friendship blossomed. As her weekly visits became a habit I relied on, I'd prepare a cool pitcher of lemonade or iced tea before she came. She would bring granola bars or her scrumptious applesauce cookies.

Now, when my alarm rings in the morning, I quickly dress with an enthusiasm not usually associated with preparing to work out. I meet my neighbor in front of my house, and together with her friendly dog, we walk around the block to the park. Then, once a week on our usual day, we do the yard work. I pull out the yard equipment and sit with Lady while Mac mows and trims.

Many seasons have come and gone since Mac and Lady came into my yard and my heart. My husband Jim once told me, "Maisy, every day you need to look forward to something." Little did I know I would find it in my own backyard.

Sophisticated Ladies

I never liked my name. Mary. So simple and plain. As a child in elementary school, I fantasized about changing my name to something more elegant and sophisticated. Something "French." And

when I befriended another imaginative, shy little girl named Mona, I found out she, too, had such fantasies.

At 7, we decided that we were no longer Mary and Mona, but rather "Patricia" and "Monique." We chose those names because they sounded mature and exotic. Maybe we just chose them because they weren't ours, but soon we had become Patricia and Monique, and we insisted that all of our classmates use our new monikers when addressing us. Most of them either laughed at us or ignored our attempts at *savoir faire* and continued to call us by our old names. Our teachers just shook their heads and wondered if this crazy idea was something that would spread to the

other children. We didn't care, for we had completely taken on our new identities. We even demanded that our family members treat us as the European sophisticates we knew we had become.

Although neither of our families could afford fancy French designer clothes, Monique and I pretended to be dressed in the finest of

fashions, and we strutted around like two little divas in denim and sneakers. At recess, we simply couldn't be bothered with such barbaric practices as kickball and hopscotch. Instead, we sat together and talked in lofty accented voices that we thought sounded so wonderful, but were probably closer to pig Latin than French. Our whole lives had changed with our identities, and suddenly we were not little girls in pigtails and ankle socks, but worldly women who possessed the manners and airs of high society. We even struck envy in other little girls our age, who had watched us with amused curiosity, but were now eager to join the fun and take on new and more glamorous personas.

Soon, we had a little club of about seven or eight girls who had gone from Jenny, Sue, and Lisa to Jonelle, Cecilia, and Evette. There must have been strength in numbers, for many of the kids who had refused to acknowledge our transformations now addressed us all

accordingly. Monique and I felt like the queens of the school, and we giggled and reveled in our newfound admiration and popularity.

I don't really remember why or when Monique and I got tired of our new identities and went back to being just Mona and Mary. I suspect it just got so exhausting trying to be something we were not, something we weren't even sure we wanted to be. I imagine it even got a little boring and tedious always having to be polite and mature and have impeccable manners, even while eating sloppy joes at the lunch table. It seems, at age 7, we learned the valuable lesson that wearing fancy clothes and talking with our pinkies held out sounded awfully exciting, but was not really more exciting than running and jumping and occasionally even getting dirty in a game of kickball. Besides, growing up could wait, but childhood could not wait.

Sometimes I think about my old friend Mona. I wonder what she is doing, where she lives, and what she must be like all these years later. Is she wearing designer dresses and speaking French as she sips lattes at an outdoor café? Or is she just like me, a simple American woman in blue jeans and a T-shirt munching on a burger and tooling around town in my SUV—proud to be exactly who I am?

A Friend in the Family

Within large families, friendships can suddenly blossom; this occurred between Ellen and Lisette. They'd known each other as part of the noisy bustle at huge family gatherings, where they exchanged casual remarks over snacks and saw each other as another face among many cousins and in-laws.

Yet, something drew them together after Lisette heard of Ellen's recent diagnosis of serious illness. They began to sit together at those huge family get-togethers, held often in sprawling backyards. And thus they shared on a deeper, more intense level than the usual family gathering chats.

When Lisette asked how Ellen was doing, she was really concerned and waited to listen to details with an awareness the rest of the family didn't have. As it turned out, Lisette's younger brother, who'd lived five states away, had suffered from the same illness. Lisette knew all the terminology, all the tests, and all the potential dangers

and risks. She'd been through them all, worrying, waiting, and praying for her brother's recovery.

Over the months of Ellen's illness and continued complications, Lisette was always there, caring, listening, and understanding. She knew exactly what Ellen was going through. They both understood the seriousness of the complications that hit Ellen, one after another, eventually sending her back into the hospital.

"I'm scared," Ellen would tell Lisette, calling late at night after the visitors had gone home and she didn't have to pretend to feel a confidence that wasn't there. She didn't have to talk about the fear she felt. Lisette heard it in her voice and always somehow found calming, strengthening, and encouraging words to offer to her dear friend.

Nightly Ellen called, and nightly Lisette helped give her courage for the struggle. They prayed together, talked about their faith, and finally said the words neither wanted to admit, but both knew were coming. They began to speak about death.

Ellen's physical strength fell steadily away. Her hands were weak and shaky, her skin almost transparent. Some days she could barely move. Visitors seemed afraid to hold her hand or touch her, as if fearing they'd catch what she had. Many didn't know what to say. Some tried cheering her up with promises that she'd recover.

Yet with Lisette, she could be real. She could speak the word "death." Together they faced what was ahead for Ellen. They searched the Bible for answers and found comfort together. They shed tears together, knowing it wouldn't be much longer now. They could see Ellen's strength draining away daily.

Then came the call Lisette had known would come. Ellen had slipped into a coma, one she wouldn't come out of.

"I'm going to see her," Lisette told her family.

"It won't matter, dear," they all told her. "She won't even know you're there. She could linger that way for months."

But Lisette went anyway. She stood close to her friend, holding her hand, studying the pale, blank face, and spoke words of courage and strength. She read a few of their favorite Bible verses and just sat awhile to be with her friend. Then she leaned close and shared something with Ellen.

"My brother died, you know. I think you always knew. I couldn't be there with him when the time came. But I wanted to be here with you."

Was it her imagination or did the limp fingers tighten around her own ever so slightly? Other visitors came then, so Lisette left. By the time she got home, her phone was ringing. Ellen was gone. Lisette missed her friend so much, but she felt somehow she'd been sent to be a strength and comfort in those last few months of Ellen's life. And that brought her comfort, too.

Building a friendship is like learning to dance. You take small, easy steps at first, then gradually add new ones until it becomes comfortable and familiar.

Put on Your Hiking Boots!

I met my friend Michael through music. We play in a band together. But as I've gotten to know Michael, our friendship has grown to be about more than just music. I don't remember how I learned that this consummate keyboard player is also an avid hiker and bicyclist, but when I did, I was happy to know that there was someone with whom I might tag along once in a while on excursions through the beauty that surrounds us in the Pacific Northwest.

Michael has dubbed me his "hikey-bikey" buddy. Generally, we plan ahead for our outings, but on sunny weekend mornings, as I work away at my computer, I'm on alert for the possibility that Michael may phone and propose that we pedal our bikes several miles before stopping for lunch and then pedaling back.

On my birthday this year, we hiked five-and-a-half miles into a mountainous area to view the beautiful Lake Valhalla. It was an 11-mile round-tripper—a mere jaunt for Michael, but an epic work-

out for me. This disparity in our strength and endurance, however, has never become an issue in our enjoyment of adventures in the great outdoors. Michael—the man who earlier in the summer hiked 80 miles among the peaks of Glacier National Park—has never made me feel like a burden or a wimp. When I thank him for not minding what I call our "girl-paced" outings, he smiles and assures me that he enjoys the "moderate" speed.

It surprises some people that my friendship with Michael is not "romantic." Rather, an innocent enjoyment of one another's company and a mutual love for God's creation characterizes our times together. Our relationship remains uncomplicated and refreshing—a nice change of pace when life becomes overwhelming.

Right now we're planning a big outing for next fall: a bike tour through New England. We hope to interest several friends in sharing the experience with us. Who knows? Maybe we'll end up forming a whole "hikey-bikey" group. Michael would get a kick out of it, and so would I.

Come what may, I hope there will always be that occasional sunny Saturday afternoon when the phone rings, and Michael's voice asks, "Whatcha doin' today?"

The Cloudburst

After an afternoon of shopping, Katie and I were caught in a sudden cloudburst. When she grabbed my hand to prevent me from running for cover, I really shouldn't have been surprised. After all, she always referred to herself as "the wild one."

So there we stood, getting thoroughly soaked. "You're crazy!" I yelled above the "plink, plink" noise of the rain hitting the cars and sidewalks.

"Yeah, well, you're all wet!" She answered back. Then raising her arms to the sky, she laughed loudly, her radiant face the only sunshine in view.

"Just look at it for what it is," she said dramatically. "The earth is taking a cool, refreshing shower after a long hot summer of sunbathing!" Then with mock earnestness, she added, "Mother Nature has extended to us the privilege of participating."

We both laughed as our makeup ran down our faces, and with it all our inhibitions washed away. We were suddenly six years old again. We splashed in puddles, kicked the rain from the gutter onto the

sidewalk, and turned our faces to the sky, catching raindrops in our mouths.

Soaking wet and smiling widely, we finally ducked under an awning, exhausted.

"Remember when we used to . . . " she began.

"Play in the sprinklers?" I finished.

"Yeah," we sighed in unison. After a smile and a brief but meaningful squeeze of our dripping hands, we parted and went our separate ways.

While I walked back to my car, my mind went back 20 years to the hot summer days of childhood. Days when Katie and I lived on the same block, just two houses apart. Days when our favorite times were spent in each other's company.

Summers were definitely the best. We usually would spend half of the day at her house and half of the day at

mine, depending on our mother's schedules. In the morning, we would always engross ourselves in a game of make-believe. We were movie stars or space princesses or cowgirls. Although each game was intricately detailed, those details changed as quickly and as often as our imaginations shifted gears.

Then it was lunchtime. We reluctantly pulled ourselves from our games, complaining and often whining because we had to stop. We never did admit to being hungry, but very soon we were just as enthusiastically engrossed in eating as we had been in playing. At Katie's house we always ate bologna sandwiches cut diagonally into four small triangles and fruit drink. At mine, it was peanut butter and jelly cut into four small square quarters and served with cold milk. Anything else beyond the sandwiches was usually ignored until coaxed or bribed into consumption.

Both Katie and I had swing sets in our backyards. After lunch we were sent outside to slide, run, climb, hang upside-down, and maybe even swing. Soon, when we were tired or hot, one of us would always think of our most favorite diversion of all. Then we would ask my mother or hers if we could play in the sprinklers.

It was inevitable—any hot summer day would eventually end with the refreshing spray of water. How we loved this simple pastime! What a wonderful treat it was to enjoy all

these small pleasures of nature! And we really enjoyed the soft grass under our bare feet, the cooling pure water readily available with the turn of the spigot, and the warm, drying rays of the sun. Even the shivers and the drippy, messy cleanup that would follow was part of the fun.

This simple childhood memory is but one of many I share with my still-best-friend Katie. It might be a song, a word, or a sigh that will spur on a particular recollection. We then smile and say once again in unison of thought and voice, "Remember when we used to . . . "

The miracle of friendship usually begins with a simple smile.

Office Mates

"That's nice, hon," Sally answered her younger son, half listening while he poured out news from his school day. Then a bit of information caught her full attention. "What? What did you say your new friend's name is?"

Ben gave her a disgusted look. "Mom, you weren't listening. His name's Sean. Remember, I told you."

"I was listening. What's his last name again?"

"Chastain, Mom. See you later, gotta go."

Sally watched him take off for a ball game at the park, but her thoughts drifted to another time, years ago, when she was younger and single and when she shared an office with a young male co-worker with that same last name. He had become a good friend. Warm memories flowed through her mind.

Shared coffee breaks. Quick lunch trips to browse used bookstores together. Taking turns treating for lunch. Making loans till payday. How many hours had she and Chad talked together after work

about relationships, their careers and personal interests, and future plans for their lives?

They'd laughed together, shared jokes, listened to one another's problems, and been good friends. So what had happened? Yes, she remembered. She had changed jobs. A great job with better money and benefits. Gradually, they had lost touch with each other, going their own ways and getting on with their lives.

All those years ago. It seemed such a long time. Surely her son hadn't made friends with her old friend's son. And yet she could hardly wait for Ben to return from the park.

"Hon, do you know anything about Sean's family? Like his dad's name?" she asked eagerly.

Ben stared at her as if she'd grown a tail or two. "His dad's name? I, uh, don't know. Why?"

"Just wondering. It wouldn't happen to be Chad, would it?"

"Yeah, that sounds right. I heard his mom and dad talking. That sounds like the name." After her son left her alone, Sally dashed for the phone.

Could it be? Had she rediscovered an old, lost friendship through her son's new friendship? The moment she heard the voice on the phone, she knew, recognizing it even after all these years.

She felt a moment of shyness, then began talking, trying to explain, "Is this Chad Chastain? The one who used to work at . . . "

"Sally? Is that you?"

And then they were both talking at once, catching up on all the misplaced years, amazed that their sons' friendship had reawakened theirs!

Sometimes the best medicine is a friend's voice on the phone.

Visiting Rhoda

The time I spent as a volunteer at a large local retirement home was the most enriching period of my adult life. I was a member of a small group of young ministers in training who went to homes for seniors who were facing the sunset of their lives alone, forgotten, and ignored.

I spent a lot of time with one elderly woman in particular, a feisty, bedridden 93 year old named Rhoda. She had no family, at least none that thought enough of her to visit, and she had outlived all her friends. At the home, everyone loved her for her sharp wit and caustic tongue. Everybody knew Rhoda, and every nurse and caregiver in the huge facility had their own fond stories of encounters with her.

I adored her and spent hours sitting by her bedside listening to stories of her colorful past. I became her best friend, and she was fast becoming mine. I often had to force myself to break away from our long and enjoyable conversations and get on with my other assignments. Rhoda would always tell me how much she missed me when I was away, and soon I was devoting so much time to her that

people were calling us mother and daughter! I know Rhoda loved that, never having had children of her own.

I loved it, too, for I had lost my own mother years before, ironically to the same type of blood cancer Rhoda was suffering from. So I welcomed this woman's friendship and planned to take full advantage of my time with her. Rhoda reciprocated by sharing with me so many of the lessons she had learned over her 93 years—some happy and some tragic, and I felt blessed to be the recipient of her guidance and advice, which often sounded harsh but was always intended with love. Rhoda had a way of looking you straight in the eye and telling you, in no uncertain terms, just what you needed to hear. I often shared my deepest fears and personal problems with her, and I never left her room without some new insight. I had many friends my own age, but none of those relationships seemed as enriching as my friendship with this unusual spirit named Rhoda. Her courage, wit, and wisdom were contagious.

As Rhoda's disease worsened, her body became like a small child's, with nothing but delicate skin covering delicate bone. I stayed with her as much as I could. It seemed the more ill she became, the more she needed to talk to me, to share with me all the love and lessons she could before it would be too late. I drank in her every word as though it were precious liquid gold.

When Rhoda passed away, it was a beautiful autumn morning. She went quietly in her sleep. As I stood in the hallway, numb with grief, I wondered if she was yelling and laughing the whole way to heaven. I imagined she would probably already be giving the angels advice in her sharp but loving way.

The entire retirement facility went into mourning. She would truly be missed, and perhaps no one would miss her more than I. Rhoda had taught me so much, given me so much, and been so much to me. She had reminded me that seniors are full of life and should be valued. I could only hope I had given as much back to her during our time together. And though my heart ached from her passing, I knew exactly what she would have wanted me to do. So, the day after she was laid to rest, I went back to the retirement home and introduced myself to a new patient—a new friend.

Date Night

"Listen," Angie said earlier over the phone, "if that new guy you met calls, we'll cancel, OK?" It was their regular weekly arrangement. Plans were never absolute. As two young women listening to their biological clocks ticking busily away, Angie and Kate kept their plans together tentative, just in case a promising date showed up at the last moment.

So Angie told herself it didn't matter that Kate wasn't there at the Italian restaurant. Usually they tried to call if they couldn't make it, but when an interesting new man arrived, each understood the other might have to cancel at the last moment, which was fine for both of them.

"It doesn't matter," Angie told herself, settling into her seat, alone, scanning the menu. But she felt very alone. Most tables were crowded with families, groups of laughing friends, thoroughly absorbed couples, even pairs of career women like herself and Kate. "No big deal," she told herself. Yet, she couldn't help feeling a bit self-conscious and uncomfortable. She should have brought a paperback book or newspaper, or some papers from work to pore over so she'd have something to do while waiting for her salad.

She didn't quite know what to do with her hands. She worked hard at tuning out the background noise of chattering diners enjoying their evening together. She reminded herself that she'd do the same if a great guy suddenly showed up. You never could tell when an eligible man might appear. After all, they were not getting any younger.

But she couldn't help feeling hurt, though she tried to ignore it. They'd been friends for ages, getting together for meals so neither had to eat alone between relationships.

Well, she wouldn't let it bother her. They had their agreement. If an interesting man showed up, their friendship went on hold. They both had wanted it that way. Her salad arrived, and she kept busy nibbling, making it last, not wanting to sit there alone with nothing to do, no one to chat with, looking pathetic and lonely. Her heart was sinking faster than a torpedoed ship.

Then, just as her pasta arrived, she caught a glimpse of Kate, pushing through the door, searching the crowded restaurant for her. She raised an arm in greeting, and Kate rushed over, breathlessly dropping into her seat. "Sorry, I'm so late," Kate apologized. "The traffic was absolutely terrible. You know how it gets. I'm glad you went ahead without me."

Angie felt a rush of pleasure that her friend had showed up. "Better late than never. But I'm so sorry that new guy didn't call you. He sounded really nice, and interesting, too. Maybe he'll still call in the next few days, right?"

Kate shifted in her chair. "Well," she told her friend, "uh, actually, he did call."

Angie stared, amazed. "What happened?"

"I got to thinking about it," Kate told her. "I got to thinking about how many times one of us has canceled because some guy shows up at the last minute. It's as though we're on hold with our lives whenever a man strolls in. I mean, new guys come and go. But our friendship is rock solid. You're always there for me. Anyway, I told him I already had plans, and he could check with me next week."

Angie felt her throat tighten up. "Yeah, I know what you mean. Having a friend to count on is worth a dozen 'hot dates.' Now, go ahead and order your pasta. I don't want to gain twenty pounds here alone."

Kate grinned. "Don't worry. I can out-pasta you any day."

I Hear You Loud and Clear

While I'm certainly not a psychic, it does amaze me that I will occasionally choose to call a dear-but-rarely-seen friend precisely on the day she needs me to call. I remember one phone call in particular to a childhood friend who had moved to Seattle three years earlier. Mindy and I had first met in kindergarten, which translates into 37 years of friendship!

Now I admit there were periods when we drifted apart—like in the sixth grade when David McKlintock asked Mindy to go steady and for the following three weeks she was always busy after school. But they broke up when David started basketball season, and Mindy and I just picked up where we left off. Then there was the time my parents enrolled me in an art class, and for two weeks I sketched only apples after school. But this eventually became tiresome, and besides, my brother ate all the apples. Mindy and I just picked up where we left off then as well. Even while attending universities at opposite ends of the country, we managed—much to our parents'

chagrin—to phone at least once a week. It seemed that no matter who or what entered our lives, we always floated back to each other's side.

So when Mindy moved to Seattle, I was sad but not miserable. We still had the phone, plus that newfangled invention that our children kindly taught us . . . e-mail! We also acquired airline credit cards, hungrily charging up points to fly back and forth. After three years, though, our frequent chats declined. In addition to the miles separating us, our respective growing families, expanding careers, and hectic lives made it even more difficult to regularly touch base. Inevitably and regretfully, our phone conversations dwindled to quarterly. I called her on her birthday, she called me on mine, and at least twice a year someone called the other with some grand announcement.

One day, however, I awoke with an overwhelming desire to call Mindy. So I did. Much to my surprise, my dear childhood friend had lost her grandmother that past evening. It had been a wonderfully close and special relationship between Mindy and her grandmother. I knew because I had shared much of their happiness. My friend and I spent 90 minutes remembering this grand woman. I cared not that I

had dialed during peak time; I didn't even mind that I'd be late for work. Mindy and I leisurely wandered back through time, sharing all sorts of recollections. Like when Mindy's grandmother took us to the circus and never once said "No" when we asked, "Can we have that?" Or the time this wonderful woman took us to the most elegant restaurant in the city, and sitting right next to us was David Cassidy from *The Partridge Family*. Mindy's grandma let us each swipe something from David's table after he left. I got his napkin, Mindy his spoon.

Now I'm certain Mindy would have called soon enough to tell me of her grandmother's passing, but somehow, some way, a true and honest friendship transcends the miles separating us, as well as the household chores demanding our attention, the office deadlines jammed in our calendars, and the car pool schedules that drive us mad. Even with all these obligations consuming our minds, I heard her call for a calming voice, someone who shared her past. I swear I had heard my friend call. Naturally, I just had to call her right back.

Fire Alarm Chili

"That's the surprise you have for me?" Janice wailed. "Your two bosses and their wives are coming here for dinner?"

"I thought you'd be thrilled," Tony said innocently. "Ever since I landed this new job, you've been asking to meet my coworkers. Bosses are coworkers."

"But, Tony, I'm just learning to cook."

"Honey, you can do anything. Besides, I want them to meet my terrific wife." Tony was smiling affectionately, and Janice couldn't refuse the wishes of her new husband.

"Oh, all right. I'll do my best. Just don't expect a gourmet meal."

Janice was determined to make the dinner a success. She took a vacation day from work to clean their apartment, shop for groceries, and cook the meal. Because she was nervous about the cooking part, she began extra early. Propping up her cookbook against the flour canister, Janice vigorously chopped piles of vegetables and began to

sauté chunks of pork in a frying pan with sweet onions. Things would be all right, she kept telling herself. The recipe was easy. Everything was under control. What could possibly go wrong? Janice was starting to feel at ease.

Just then the phone rang in the living room. It was a telemarketer intent on selling her a long-distance phone service. He refused to accept Janice's polite "No, thank you," and was trying to keep her on the line. Janice was so frustrated that she didn't notice the huge billows of black smoke wafting out from her kitchen. Then she heard the smoke detector's frantic beep.

"My kitchen's on fire!" she screamed.

Flames were leaping out of the frying pan. Thinking quickly, Janice threw a box of baking soda into the charred mess that had once been tender bites of pork. This put out the fire, and a sharp whack with a broom handle shut off the smoke detector, but the tiny apartment was so filled with smoke that Janice couldn't breathe.

A few minutes later Mrs. Arnette, the next-door neighbor, spotted Janice sitting outside on the fire escape, sobbing.

"What in the world's going on?" Mrs. Arnette demanded, sticking her head through the window.

Janice had seen Mrs. Arnette in passing a few times since they'd moved into the building. She had thought the fiftyish woman in her elegant designer clothing and perfectly styled hair might be snobbish, but now Janice needed to tell someone about her troubles.

"You were trying to make chili con carne, but it looks like you made fire alarm chili instead," the older woman chuckled. "Don't feel bad, honey. Learning to cook—everyone has to start off with a few mistakes. I have my own restaurant now—Nicolette's downtown—"

"Oh! That fancy French place? The food there is incredible!"

"Thanks, but I couldn't cook when I was first married, either. Here's a dark secret: I served my in-laws a roast chicken with the giblets still inside—wrapped in paper!"

Janice couldn't help smiling.

"We need to air your place out and get to work. There's still time to make a nice dinner before your guests arrive."

Janice couldn't believe what Mrs. Arnette was saying to her. "You mean you'd help me?" she asked wide-eyed.

"Sure. Between your refrigerator and mine, there must be enough ingredients for a passable meal."

Tony was surprised at the tasty hors d'oeuvres Janice brought out to their guests. He was puzzled at the elegantly set table and frankly amazed at the delicious soup. But when an attractive middle-aged woman appeared, carrying the main course, he was speechless.

"I'm a friend of Janice's," Mrs. Arnette stated. "I offered to lend an extra pair of hands tonight, since this is her first dinner party."

"I'm still learning to cook," Janice smiled, giving her new friend a little hug. "But I'm making progress. After all, I'm taking lessons from a genuine French chef!"

Friendship usually begins with two people discovering their similarities, but the relationship is firmly established when they learn to appreciate each other's differences.

Can You Forgive Me?

"Don't tell anyone, promise?" That's what my friend Kristy asked when she told me a secret about her family—something exceedingly painful and private, something she'd never told anyone before, something she didn't want anyone else to ever hear.

I don't know what happened to me. I don't know how it happened. I never meant to tell anyone. Somehow it just slipped out. I've asked myself a thousand times since then how I could have done it, how I could have betrayed my friend, how I could have let a secret so private and hurtful for her get away from me. I can't quite believe I did something so totally unforgivable.

I betrayed my friend, failed her, let her down when it counted most. She'd trusted me as she'd never trusted anyone before, and I opened my mouth like a complete idiot and gave away her trust. I just started talking to another friend and then the secret slipped out. I thought maybe it would be OK, that nobody else would hear

about it, and that it wouldn't go any further. But the next thing I knew, everybody was talking. I overheard conversations about Kristy's home life almost everywhere I went. Her private experiences were public knowledge, and it was all my fault.

Realizing what I'd done, I wanted to hide and never face her again. She must hate me. She'd have to know it was me. I was the only person she ever told. So how else could her private life have become public gossip? And she would have heard by now. I knew people were talking about her, staring at her, whispering when she walked past. I couldn't stand thinking about it.

It made me feel sick deep inside. I wished I could have taken back my foolish words and never let them loose. But words once spoken can't be undone. It was too late. I felt like crying. I'd betrayed my friend and made her life miserable.

Could Kristy ever forgive me? By opening my stupid mouth at the worst time, had I destroyed our friendship? I felt like crying every time I thought about what I'd done. I wanted to run away and disappear, never to be seen again. I didn't want to meet Kristy face to

face and look into her eyes. I knew what I'd see there—hurt, shock, and probably plenty of anger.

I'd never felt so terrible in my entire life. But this was my friend. I had to do something. I had to go to her and tell her how sorry I was, how stupid I'd been, that I hadn't meant to break her trust. It took all my courage and more to force myself to go to her house. My hands shook. My stomach clenched up. It was the hardest trip I'd ever made, and when I got to her house, I thought I wouldn't be able to walk up to the door and knock. How could I face her? What would I say?

I started thinking how I'd feel if she'd done this to me. Could I forgive her? I wasn't sure.

I stood in front of her door; I worked up the courage to knock but wanted to run the moment the door started to open. How could I face her? Then I saw the look in her eyes.

"I'm so sorry," I said. But before I could say much more, she reached for me, hugging hard, and I hugged her back. We stood that way, sobbing and leaning on one another, and I knew she understood and forgave and that we were still friends.

Miss Priss

One April morning when I opened my back door, I noticed mist rising up from the grass. Suddenly a Persian cat, silver-gray like the mist, stepped out of nowhere and walked purposefully into my kitchen. She proceeded to tour my townhouse with uplifted head as if she were a queen visiting the common people. Then she leapt onto the kitchen counter and looked at me with calm amber eyes.

"Perhaps your majesty would be interested in breakfast?" I asked. Opening a can of tuna, I offered her some on a saucer. She sniffed it, thought about it for a minute, and finally ate the morsel in small, delicate bites.

"You're not wearing a collar. I wonder if you're lost. Do you need a new home, kitty?" Ignoring me, the cat jumped onto a nearby window seat and curled up for a snooze on the gingham cushion. "I think I should call you Miss Priss," I decided, "because of those lofty airs you put on. Well, you can stay here if you like. I could use some company."

But Miss Priss held her own firm opinions about having a new home. Sometimes she would visit me for several days in a row. Then

she would disappear for two or three days, turning up suddenly when I thought she was gone for good. I had no idea where she spent her time away from me until one evening, when I was taking my trash out to the Dumpster, I saw the cat coming out of a townhouse two doors down from mine.

"Excuse me," I called. "It's Mrs. Freemont, isn't it? I'm Cecilia Whitford."

"Hi, neighbor," she said, walking over to me. "Call me Mitzi."

"The cat that just came out of your place—does she belong to you?"

"No. She just comes to visit. She stays for a few days, then disappears for a while. Why?"

"Well, she spends a lot of time at my place, too. She's not exactly mine, either, but I guess I'm used to having her around."

Miss Priss was weaving herself between our ankles, rubbing against first one of us, then the other. She purred loudly.

"So Fluffy, you're staying with this lady, too, eh?" Mitzi questioned the cat, who showed no signs of having been disloyal to either of us. Mitzi then bent down to scratch the cat's chin. "Well, we're on to you now! You're a two-timer!"

I was disappointed in Miss Priss when I discovered she was visiting Mitzi Freemont. Mitzi's lifestyle wasn't as quiet and dignified as I felt a senior citizen's should be. True, I didn't know a great deal about her, only that she was a widow like me and around my age. Unlike me, she had a large family and a sizable group of friends. As I lay in bed late at night I often heard car doors, laughter, and squealing children.

Later when Miss Priss was gone for nearly a week, I became extremely worried about her. After thinking it over, I hurried down the lane to Mitzi's place. "Hi, Cecilia," she said. "What's up?"

"It's Miss Priss—I mean the gray cat," I said awkwardly. "I haven't seen her since last Thursday. I was wondering if she's been to your place since then."

"No, I haven't seen her either, and I've been worried, too. Come on in." As she poured me a mug of coffee, she suggested, "Maybe it's time to start looking for her. I know what: We'll mount a neighborhood search!"

Before the day was over, Mitzi had 17 people doing door-to-door searches for our missing kitty. Just before suppertime there was a knock at my own door. I opened it to find Mitzi with her grandson

Drake, who was holding an indignant-looking silver-gray Persian cat.

"Miss Priss!" I shouted. I tried to sound angry, but I was really relieved to see her.

"She's been on vacation," Drake laughed. "Last week the Petersons on the next block were loading up their van for a trip to their cottage. The cat must have jumped in when they weren't looking, because she went along for the ride. She just got home."

"Cecilia," Mitzi said, "I think we should buy a collar for this naughty kitty with two tags on it—one with your address, and one with mine. I guess we'd better agree on a name for her, too. I think your name fits her better. Miss Priss. She does act like royalty!"

That evening I found myself at a potluck dinner in Mitzi's townhouse. As I sat in the crowded kitchen, surrounded by her welcoming family and friends, I realized why I'd disapproved of Mitzi. I envied her because she was leading a full and happy life. And I knew that now she intended to include me in it.

Miss Priss sat on a windowsill, placidly cleaning her toes as if she knew very well that she had just changed my entire world.

A Window of Opportunity

I have old friends (as in grade school chums), and I have borrowed friends (as in my husband's best friends' wives), and I have office friends (as in by-the-coffee-pot work acquaintances), but once in a while I make a new friend who fills a remarkable gap in my life—a gap I previously never knew existed. Such is the story about Annette, a woman who lives across the street from me and who became a very special friend.

I first met Annette about three weeks after she and her family moved in. While I stood in my living room by the bay window one blustery winter morning, I spotted this woman carrying a large pink puffy bundle in her arms. Since she hugged this parcel with delicate affection, I assumed the best. "Gee," I commented to Anna, my 17-month-old daughter, "That woman appears to be carrying a child about your age. And by the look of the child's pink snowsuit, it's a girl."

I looked at my daughter blowing bubbles and took that as a positive sign. So we bundled ourselves up and wandered across the road. I knocked on this woman's door and introduced myself. She welcomed me into her home, introduced herself, and then produced her 23-month-old daughter, Jasmine. We chatted a bit, watched the two toddlers observe each other, and finally made plans to visit a children's museum the following week. It was the first step toward what was to become a double friendship.

Two little girls grew into inseparable buddies, wandering in and out of each other's homes with total ease. When my daughter's kindergarten teacher asked each student to create a collage of family photographs, Anna naturally included a picture of Jasmine. When Anna burst out crying one day because she hated all her clothes, Jasmine brought over her best jumper with all the ruffles and embroidered roses. These two little girls never really set up plans; they simply crossed the street as if a giant, invisible tunnel connected their two homes.

Two women also grew together, facing the perils and joys of motherhood with one another's complete support. Here was a woman to worry with while we watched our daughters grow, to

concur with about curfews, and to brag to about great and glorious school grades. As the years and phases passed far too quickly, we assured one another that this situation or that predicament was normal, affirming the fact that I was never alone in my concerns and she was never silly in her fears.

We didn't discuss only anxieties, however; we also laughed. Annette soon picked up on my nervous ways, obsessing about Anna's every little development. And she enjoyed every possible opportunity to tease me about my worries. Likewise, I was eventually able to joke with Annette about her seemingly endless preoccupation with Jasmine's social activities. Of course, after making wisecracks, I always wanted to see the most recent pictures of Jasmine. It was a comfort, having Annette close by.

It seems I had the old friends to remember days gone by, the borrowed friends to chat with about our husbands' antics, and the office friends to analyze perplexing 9-to-5 politics; but I had no mommy friends until that blustery winter morning when I wandered over to Annette's home. This was a friend I never knew I needed . . . until we met. You know, I look forward to the day when we will take our friendship to the next level. I look forward to the day I will watch her through my living room bay window, coming over for coffee so we can share photos of our grandkids.

Paint Job

It had been nearly seven hours since the ambulance took Mark Owens away. His wife, Loretta, had followed with their car, leaving in such a hurry that no one in the neighborhood had a chance to ask her what was wrong. While Betty cleared away the dishes from dinner, she heard the crunch of tires in her neighbors' driveway. Picking up the phone, she speed-dialed their friend Fran across the street.

"Loretta's finally home," she said. "See you over there."

Hastily she picked up a casserole dish and sprinted out the door. Fran joined her with half of a blueberry pie. Together they greeted their friend as she slid out of the driver's seat.

"Loretta! What happened to Mark?" Betty asked. "Is he going to be all right?"

Their neighbor closed the car door and turned toward them, relieved to see friendly faces. "He had a heart attack! He's going to be OK, but he'll be in the hospital for at least a few days."

"Thank heaven he'll be all right!" Fran breathed. "We've been worried ever since we saw you leave. Is there anything we can do to help?"

"Not really. I called our family from the hospital. I'm just going to get something to eat and go to bed." There were dark circles of fatigue around Loretta's eyes.

"Here's some tuna casserole and a little dessert. At least you won't have to cook tonight."

"Thanks, guys. That's really thoughtful."

As Loretta turned to open her front door, she exclaimed, "Oh, no!"

"What's the matter?" Betty asked.

"Look at this notice! It was left on our front door. The city is citing us for the peeling paint on our house." With a sigh, Loretta slumped onto the top porch step. "That's all we need right now."

"Maybe you could call and explain. I'm sure they'd understand and give you an extension," Fran suggested.

"Not this time. You know Mark. He's a sweetheart, but he's felt really tired lately. He bought the paint months ago. The cans are stacked up in the garage, but he hasn't been motivated to get out there and do the work. The city's losing patience with us. They've already given us two extensions."

Her friends exchanged glances. "Why don't you let some of us in the neighborhood help you paint?" Betty offered.

"No. I really couldn't ask you to do that," Loretta said firmly. "I'll just have to start painting as soon as Mark's able to come home from the hospital."

The next morning, right after Loretta left for the hospital, an oddly dressed group of neighbors gathered on her lawn. About 15 people

of various ages, from small children to senior citizens, arrived wearing ragged or paint-stained clothing. Betty set up a card table with a coffeepot and a platter of doughnuts. Fran handed out buckets of paint and brushes. Before long, everyone was at work scraping off flaking paint and brushing on a fresh coat of white.

That evening when Loretta pulled into the driveway, she was astonished to see a glittering white house with bright red trim—and a yard full of neighbors who had set up barbecue grills and folding tables. Paint-splattered adults ate hamburgers and potato salad while children played on the lawn.

Loretta stood staring beside her car for so long that Betty and Fran finally came over.

"Are you mad at us?" Fran asked.

Loretta smiled through a film of tears. "Mad at you! You saved my life! I don't know how I could have done it myself. . . . " At a loss for words, she put one arm around each of her friends and gave them a long hug.

If not for the wealth of my friendships, indeed, I would be poor.

Out of Sight, In My Mind

By my junior year in college, I had gone through two majors, three campus addresses, and four boyfriends—but only one roommate. Gwen Schplinkerman. A university computer had originally placed us in the same room, but from that chance pairing, a friendship grew, and we continued to live together even after moving out of student housing and into our own apartment.

We were an odd match—she much livelier and spontaneous than I, while I more philosophical and pensive than she, and yet we complemented each other. Even our study habits balanced out, with Gwen better at research and I more adept at the writing. Sometimes we even signed up for the same class, teaming up on projects whenever possible. First, Gwen ferreted out the facts while I handled pizza orders and phone messages. Then I wrote the paper, while she brought in Chinese food and did the laundry. We aced those projects every time. On graduation day we

each received a degree as well as a heartfelt promise to remain friends forever.

Twenty-eight years later I found myself still fondly remembering my dear college friend, but sadly I didn't have a clue where she lived, what she was up to, or even what her last name was. I vaguely recalled hearing that she got married sometime in the late 1970s, but to whom I no longer recalled.

One day, my 17-year-old daughter looked up from her college directory and began to ask questions about my collegiate career. One thing lead to another, and before I knew it, we had pulled out my college memory box. Out tumbled a young girl's past—matchbook covers, Ft. Lauderdale motel room keys, plus lots and lots of amusing photographs. As my daughter and I sorted through the pictures, a dramatic black-and-white portrait of a beautiful woman fell off to the side.

"Who's this?" my daughter asked.

"That's Gwen, my college roommate, a wonderful friend."

"Why haven't I ever met her?" my daughter continued.

"Because we drifted apart. That's life, I guess," I remarked quite sadly. "We drifted apart."

That night, after the kitchen was clean, the homework done, and the next day's lunches made, my mind wandered back to Gwen. Why had I let such a terrific friendship slip through the cracks? What would she be like today? Did she have any children? I couldn't shake the questions. As I made my way upstairs, I passed the spare bedroom—the room we'd recently turned into a computer room. Much to my surprise, the computer lay idle. No kids e-mailing other kids or frantic last-minute term papers lighting the screen.

I decided to try one of those incredible Internet searches for my old roommate, but the only information I had was Gwen's maiden name—Schplinkerman. How many Schplinkerman's could there be in this world? Sure enough I found one—Jeffrey Schplinkerman in Manhattan. If memory served correctly, that was the name of my dear friend's brother. So I e-mailed Jeffrey Schplinkerman in Manhattan. I explained that I was looking for Gwen Schplinkerman and that I suspected she might be his sister. I guaranteed Jeffrey that I was not some weird stalker, tracking his sister, but rather a one-time close friend wanting to reconnect. If Gwen was indeed his sister, could he please send me Gwen's e-mail address?

Two days later I received a response. He simply asked, "What color is Gwen's hair?" Not an odd question since Gwen had always been known for her amazing strawberry blonde hair—the answer he was looking for. The next day

Jeffrey sent me another e-mail, including Gwen's phone number and a warm closing message, "She's anxiously waiting to hear from you."

I dialed Gwen, and a young boy answered the phone. I felt this enormous surge of utter delight. She has a son! When Gwen finally took the receiver, I felt the years—the decades—melt away. She still had that sexy raspy voice I'd always envied, and her wonderfully infectious laugh still tickled me into giggles.

"I'd forgotten how funny you are," Gwen said. "Just hearing your voice, though, gives me the incredible urge to eat pizza!"

And so it went for 40 minutes, me talking about my two daughters, she chatting about her two sons, both of us trying to cover 28 years. Oddly enough, we were each immersed in the same remodeling project—updating our respective kitchens. True to form, Gwen offered to send me gobs of research concerning the latest this or the most current that. She was, however, having trouble pulling this information into one cohesive floor plan. I, on the other hand, had tons of information on efficient floor plans, but no clue as to which refrigerator or stove to choose. It felt like old times, she helping me get started, me helping her finish the job. I guess some friendships don't really need constant care and feeding. They live on forever—no matter which way life takes you.

Weigh to Go

Ceiling fans spun energetically over banks of machines, but what struck the smattering of exercisers most was the intensity of the music blaring across the gym. Boom-badda-badda-badda-boom, the backbeat pounded. Its tempo was intended to inspire exercisers, but Margaret found it extremely irritating.

She wasn't the only person annoyed by the amplified percussion. The man puffing away to her right thrust his arms into the air and groaned, "I hate this music, and I really hate this machine."

Margaret laughed—something she had never done while exercising. "Hear you loud and clear," she responded, looking in his direction. "If this song doesn't end soon, I'm pounding a free weight into the sound system."

"Let me help you," he offered, adding, "I'm Jerry."

"Maggie," she replied.

"Are you a member?" he asked while streams of sweat poured down his puffy crimson face.

"Two years," she answered, stopping not only to chat but also to enjoy a break from her hated treadmill.

He glanced over at her. "How's it workin' for you?"

"I've lost eighty pounds."

"No way!" he exclaimed, stumbling slightly at her declaration.

"Yup," she assured him, "twenty pounds, four times."

"Tell me about it," he commiserated. "I've been up and down so many suit sizes, I have separate closets for each."

"Your wife must be relegated to the linen closet," Maggie responded.

"No wife. You?"

"No wife either."

Jerry's laugh was rich and deep. He laughed sporadically at her retort until he shut down his machine and headed for the shower. "Don't start vandalizing those speakers," he warned her. "Have fun."

When they next saw each other, Maggie and Jerry picked adjoining treadmills and resumed their chat. At the end of their workout, they made an informal exercising pact. No pressure, just a little encouragement between two friends, both of whom loved a little challenge.

It didn't take long for Maggie to realize that partnering with Jerry pushed her confidence to new heights. Their friendship gave her a sense of grounding—a feeling she had never before experienced with a man. Her lifelong battle with weight had made her vulnerable, but Jerry didn't judge. He simply accepted.

As for Jerry, he adored Maggie's spirit and dry sense of humor, while she appreciated his easygoing nature and refusal to physically tether himself to a career 24 hours a day. In sum, the two discovered they could exchange honest opinions, thoughts, hopes, and dreams. Their friendship felt like the safest place in the entire world.

As the year progressed, their commitment to exercising together was as predictable as the chimes on Big Ben. Perhaps that's why Maggie was caught off guard the morning Jerry didn't arrive at the gym at their usual time. She called his apartment, but received no answer. Perplexed, she changed into her sweats and wandered over to the treadmill area.

That's where she discovered "her" treadmill decorated with fresh red roses.

The sight made Maggie gasp—a reaction Jerry, strolling casually on the adjacent treadmill, had waited all morning to see. "Happy Anniversary, Skinny," he said. "In case you don't keep track, excuse the pun, we met one year ago today in this very spot!"

Maggie made the connection, then laughed out loud, remembering their first introduction. "You are such a treasure," she said, luxuriating in the bond the two had formed.

"True," he answered, "so how come I'm not married?"

"God is saving you for someone special," Maggie responded, gathering the flowers into the vase Jerry had left beside the treadmill. "Until then, Jerry, you're stuck with me."

She pushed the start button, and the two began to pace each other, quickly falling into a rhythm that perfectly mirrored the pace of their strong, unwavering friendship.

Unlikely Soul Mates

Carol's 27; I'm 44. She has her eye on the corner office; I have my eye on the dust bunny in the corner of my living room. She knows how to mix a great martini; I know how to mix grape juice. She likes to decorate with fragile glass objet d'art from the 1930s; I prefer child-proof, indestructible plastic. She and I have very little in common . . . except a wonderfully warm and giving friendship.

It is a most unlikely friendship, but one I treasure nonetheless. Even the circumstances under which we met are intriguing to me. Because Carol's last name is Jonus and my last name is Jones, the dry cleaners inadvertently gave her the handmade heirloom quilt Grandma stitched for me, and I got her black Armani suit with the matching cashmere sweater. After we met at the dry cleaners to rescue our respective belongings, we had each decided independently to run next door and grab some coffee to go. For some mysterious reason, still unknown to me, we did not

go. Instead, we sat. We talked. She complimented the fine needlework on my grandmother's quilt, and I positively lusted after her gorgeous cashmere sweater. For some mysterious reason, also unknown to me, we exchanged phone numbers. That was more than two years ago.

Today we share a refreshing friendship. Carol taps into my young, romantic, impetuous side, encouraging me to be wild and crazy—like the time she pressed me to put golden streaks in my hair. My husband found it appealing, my daughter thought it cool, and I felt great. I, on the other hand, keep her focused on reality, growth, and winning a lot without losing it all. Like the time I helped her see that her mother does not begrudge her professional success nor think Carol a failure because she's not married with children; Carol's mother just doesn't comprehend the drive to climb a corporate ladder. (Being influenced by equal parts June Cleaver, Mary Richards, and Ally McBeal sometimes helps me see all sides.)

Carol and I also enjoy exploring the other's latest concern—so unlike the worries we have about our own lives. When she listened to my humdrum stories about finding the right kindergarten for my daughter, she was genuinely moved, even taking the time to do research on the Internet and e-mailing me results. I haven't yet mas-

tered the Internet, and much to my friend's credit, she never once has chastised me for continuing to live in some previous decade.

Meanwhile, I listen to Carol's woes about pulling off the perfect cocktail party, and I'm honestly interested—even taking the time to clip and mail a few articles on the perfect and most appropriate appetizer menu, gathered from the many home magazines I buy and read, but never actually put to good use. And oftentimes we bridge the gap between where she's going and where I've been. For Christmas last year, I gave her a beautiful handmade quilt, one I actually created myself. She gave me a cashmere sweater, as well as an invitation to her holiday cocktail party, so I actually had someplace to wear my sweater.

Carol is living proof that a soul mate extends far beyond romantic tales of one woman and one man. A soul mate can be any person who seems, for no apparent reason, to understand your spirit, to appreciate your essence, and to value your existence. A soul mate likes you just the way you are. And so it is with my friend, Carol—my soul mate.

Threesome

"Hey, let me do those," Amy offered, quickly gathering up the dirty dishes.

Pam put up a brief, polite struggle, but then she grinned and said, "Sure, why not?"

While they passed dishes back and forth, Amy felt a flood tide of emotion, thankful for Pam and James—the nicest couple she'd ever met, feeling a sense of belonging and a part of their lives. What would she do without them? Being single when all your friends are married and busy with their own lives can be incredibly lonely. In Pam and James's home, she was filled with a sense of well-being, comfort, and warmth, but what if they became tired of her? What if all this sense of being a part of their family vanished?

She turned to Pam, her eyes uncertain and her voice anxious. "Uh, listen, I have to ask. I love being here. I mean it's great that you guys invite me so much. You make me feel a part of your family. I guess I'm thinking I don't want to wear you guys out and hang around too much, you know?"

She held the freshly washed dish in both hands, holding her breath, waiting for Pam's response.

Pam grinned. "Amy, you're the little sister I always wished I didn't have!" Then she saw how uneasy Amy was. "Don't worry, sweetie, you *are* family. I wouldn't tease you so much otherwise. And James feels the same way. Listen, Amy, I was single once. So was James. Amazingly, we had that in common." Amy smiled a little.

"Anyway," Pam continued, "I felt so alone when I was single. All my friends got married and were suddenly too busy for me. But one couple sort of adopted me. They opened up their home and their hearts to me. They kept me from feeling lonely. I even met James in their home. But he says I can't hold them responsible for that!"

Leaning close, Pam wrapped both arms around her friend. "I guess I just wanted to pass it on to you. OK?"

Amy felt the anxiety drain out of her. Then they heard a knock at the front door. "Hey," she told Pam. "I wouldn't mind a little match-making myself."

"No kidding! Well, I just happened to invite a gorgeous single man over for coffee. So go answer the door, and don't let him get away."

A Tropical Getaway

Carrie and Sally had done everything together for many years. They were best friends since college and were married within a year of each other. Their husbands even became good friends, and so the two couples spent a lot of time together. When Carrie's marriage faltered, finally ending in a painful divorce, however, she was certain it would also mean the end of her friendship with Sally, whose own marriage was solid and loving.

Fearing rejection, she pulled away from Sally, not calling her back or meeting her for lunches. When Sally would contact her, Carrie would be strangely distant and cold. Sally suspected something was terribly wrong, so she invited Carrie to a heart-to-heart dinner during which Carrie finally confessed her fear about possibly losing her friend.

Sally tried to convince Carrie that her marital status had nothing to do with their friendship, but Carrie wouldn't believe it. Therefore, to

help Carrie understand just how much she meant to Sally, Sally presented Carrie with an envelope containing a special surprise—two round-trip tickets to Hawaii for just the two of them. Carrie objected at first, saying she was just too depressed and that Sally shouldn't have spent the money, but Sally would hear nothing of it. Within the month they had re-arranged their work schedules and were on their way to the island paradise.

They stayed at a lovely resort hotel and immediately hit the sun and sand to sip yummy tropical concoctions, and thus they renewed the special bond of their friendship. It was a wonderful opportunity for the two of them to rediscover their commonalties and commiserate over their differences, including Carrie's newfound marital status. Over the next few days, they indulged in shopping, swimming, and sightseeing, and their evenings were spent sampling the wonderful array of restaurants along the beachfront.

On their fourth night there, Sally dragged Carrie to a wonderful club and even got Carrie to dance with an attractive man. Carrie was uncomfortable at first, but then she was thrilled to discover that he was from her hometown. They even exchanged phone numbers, planning to contact each other back on the mainland. Carrie realized that life did not end with divorce. In fact, in many ways, her life was beginning anew, and she had Sally to thank for reminding her that she could go on with her life.

Sally was surprised when Carrie turned down two more dancing and dinner offers with attractive men to spend the rest of her time with her friend. Carrie was excited by the attention and the much-needed boost to her self-esteem, but she realized that the truly important thing was having such a wonderful and caring friend as Sally—someone who would go to the extent of taking her on a trip to Hawaii to show her how important the bond between them would always be.

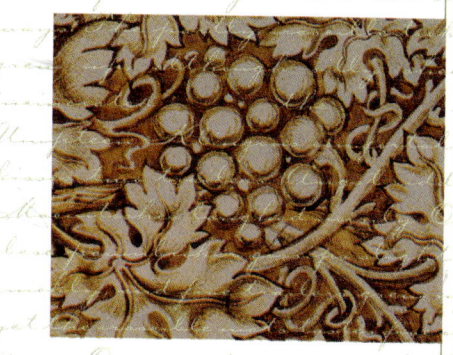

On the final day of their rejuvenating vacation, Sally and Carrie indulged in something they had both deprived themselves of for years—total pampering at a local salon. Together they allowed themselves to be treated like queens, giggling and smiling at each other like two schoolgirls.

The morning they boarded their plane for home, both women had been renewed and transformed by their time together and were already making plans to do it again the following year—just the two of them.

The Friendship Path

Now that we had been neighbors for 20 years, I wanted to give Sarah a really special birthday gift. Because she had helped me through some of the most difficult times in my life, I wanted it to be something significant and symbolic of our friendship.

I knew Sarah well enough to know any show of attention would embarrass her, so my gift could not be too ostentatious. I knew a balloon or floral bouquet wouldn't do. She would think jewelry or clothing inappropriate. She would feel badly if I spent too much money, and if it came from a store at all, she would most likely take it back. I had to find something simple—a gift from the heart.

You'd think after all these years I'd be sure to find just the right gift, but I shopped for most of two Saturdays, perused the cata-

logues, even bought a craft magazine for ideas, and still I found myself empty handed.

We had met while classmates in a beginning computer class at the local junior college. Soon we found that we had much in common. We studied together, graduated together, and eventually found our first jobs with the same company. We had become best of friends before either of us was married. We had been the maid of honor at each other's weddings, kept in close touch while I was out of state for my husband's internship, and then chose homes in the same new development—actually, side by side.

Thinking back on all we had shared together spurred my imagination. At last I had my idea. It would be perfect! Sarah would be at her parents' home for the entire weekend, and I could have her yard all to myself. I dived into my project enthusiastically, and even enlisted my husband, Neal, to help. First, we drew up some simple plans. Friday evening I bought paving stones, and early Saturday morning I began my work.

How often had Sarah commented on the hideous muddy pathway leading from her house to mine? My gift would be this: I would call this area our Friendship Path, and each stepping stone I laid would commemorate a significant event in our lives that we have shared with each other.

Carefully I dug depressions in the soil and installed the decorative rocklike pavers. Feeling creative and a little philosophical, I even wrote a poem, which I later gave to her, for each stone I selected.

The first stone was for our mutual dislike of homework and our hard-earned B's at school. The next was for helping me with my wedding, and the third was for her wedding. We quit smoking and tried to keep off the ensuing pounds together, so two more stones were installed accordingly. There were several stones representing times while we lived apart, and stones marking the births of our first children. While I laid a certain decorative stone, I smiled as I remembered how she helped me decorate my nursery. That was a special stone for a special event.

The path kept growing; there was a stone for when she was bedridden with her first pregnancy and I brought her food and company. Ones for when she watched my kids while I went to be with my mother during her illness, and when she comforted and helped me after my mother died. Stones were laid to represent the remodeling of her house to include a home office when she decided to quit work to raise her two children; her struggle with her son's learning disability; and my breast cancer scare.

While I worked, I recalled the times I advised Sarah when she confided in me about the abuse she suffered. I helped her find a counselor, and eventually I was there for her during her divorce.

And I laid a special stone for an event two years later when I introduced her to a friend of Neal's. I was matron of honor at her marriage to her beloved Paul.

Finally, the Friendship Path was complete—just as our friendship is complete. Sarah is like the sister I never had, a friend the way I always imagined a best friend should be. She's always there when I need her, and she knows when that is, whether I ask or not.

I stood back and admired the path. Then, I realized it needed one more stone. This final stone would represent all the memories, the challenges, and the accomplishments yet to be shared.

Sarah was crying when she called me the next morning. "How will I ever repay you for such a kind and thoughtful deed?" she asked through her grateful tears. But I explained that the little path I made was really just the bow on the package of the real gift—the gift of friendship she had given to me all these years.

Good friends are like good windows—they let in the light and keep out the rain.

Friendship Knows No Age

Ava had no idea when she began to work as a private nurse for the wealthy Mrs. Evie Bagwell that she would someday become more than just a caregiver to a woman dying of cancer. She would become her best friend. Their relationship began five years ago when Mrs. Bagwell was admitted to the hospital on her 75th birthday with stomach cancer. She had surgery and went through disabling chemo sessions before she was permitted to recover in her lavish upstate New York home, but only if she had a private nurse on duty. With no children of her own to care for her, Mrs. Bagwell hired Ava from a nurse's agency. She could easily afford it, having been left several million dollars by her late husband, a newspaper and magazine publisher.

At first, Ava, who was 45 years younger and from a much less advantaged background, had difficulty dealing with such a demanding perfectionist as Mrs. Bagwell. Even in her weakest moments, the older woman demanded attention and care like an army sergeant

giving orders. During quieter moments when Mrs. Bagwell was more relaxed, personal conversation was stilted, due to the gap in their ages and experiences. But as the days went on, Mrs. Bagwell accepted Ava not only into her home but also into her heart. She opened up to the young nurse, telling stories of her life and sharing wishes, dreams, and regrets about never having children. In time, Mrs. Bagwell became quite attached to Ava.

Ava, who had recently married and was looking forward to starting a family, opened up as well, and soon they were good friends and confidantes. When another round of surgery was in order, Ava brightened Mrs. Bagwell's day with the news that she was pregnant. It was enough to cheer the old woman up, and soon Mrs. Bagwell was back at home for another long period of rest and recovery. As Ava's pregnancy advanced, she and Mrs. Bagwell made all sorts of plans for the baby. Ava loved to watch the sparkle in Mrs. Bagwell's eyes when she talked about her love of children and the joy of holding a baby. Ava secretly hoped that the older woman would live long enough to hold the baby she was carrying. Mrs. Bagwell's health was slipping, although the older woman did her best to hide her pain behind a cheerful façade.

One day, Mrs. Bagwell had been suffering from intense pain that did not diminish, even with her medication. Ava had told Mrs. Bagwell she would stay overnight, but the old woman insisted she would be OK and that the night nurse would be arriving soon. So Ava went home to her husband.

The next day, Ava arrived to see an ambulance parked outside the house, and her heart sank to the ground. Inside, the paramedics were lifting Mrs. Bagwell out of bed. Ava followed the ambulance to the hospital and waited outside the surgery room for six hours. When she was finally allowed in to see her weary friend, Ava seated herself beside Mrs. Bagwell's bed in the recovery room. The old woman stirred in her sleep and awoke, gazing at Ava with tearful, loving eyes. She whispered for Ava to come closer. Mrs. Bagwell told her that she loved her and that she would never forget her. Then she told Ava something that filled her heart to bursting. "I always dreamed of having a daughter. And now I have you."

Mrs. Bagwell passed away the next morning, but her memory and her love for Ava did not end there, for Mrs. Bagwell had left most of her money to Ava and her growing family. And, to say thank you, Ava named her beautiful daughter Evie after Mrs. Bagwell, her dear patient and friend.